BRITISH STEAM
THE CLASSIC YEARS

BRITISH STEAM
THE CLASSIC YEARS

JOHN WESTWOOD

NELSON

BISON GROUP

First published in 1989 by
Bison Books Ltd
Kimbolton House
117A Fulham Road
London SW3 6RL

ISBN 0-86124-555-5

Printed in Spain by Gráficas Estella, S.A. Navarra.

10 9 8 7 6 5 4 3 2 1

PAGE 1: Duchess of
Hamilton *leaves York
Station.*

PAGES 2-3: Sir Nigel
Gresley *and* Lord Nelson *in
steam in Carnforth yard.*

BELOW: Kolhapur *making a
strong effort near Horton-in-
Ribblesdale.*

Contents

THE VICTORIAN TRAIN

LEFT: *The famous Great Northern No. 1 at work on the present day Great Central Railway.*

THE VICTORIAN TRAIN

In 1848 the Great Western Railway decided to prove the superiority of its broad gauge by staging a high-speed run from its Paddington terminus in London to Didcot, 53 miles away. The GWR train did this trip in just under 48 minutes, and the average speed of 67mph remained a British record for almost 50 years.

It is not quite as surprising as it seems that a half-century should elapse before this start-to-stop average speed was surpassed. A sizeable part of the travelling public simply did not want high speed, and it was common knowledge that trains might collide or derail and that a crash at 20mph was much less lethal than one at 50 mph. So at a time when the railways saw the need to persuade more people to travel there seemed little point in scaring them with high speeds. Inducements, such as making their trip more comfortable or, as a last resort, making it cheaper, were far more effective.

It was not until the last quarter of the century that the railways needed to provide both increased comfort and faster trains in order to attract passengers to their services. Competition between railways was developing, for by that time about 15 dominant companies had been formed from amalgamations of smaller lines, and they were each striving to better their positions by luring traffic from other railways. Few big cities in Britain had one railway as a monopoly. It was more usual for two cities to be joined by two or more lines, of which one was more direct than the others. The companies which were least favourably placed did not rely simply on advertising to increase their market share, but rather provided genuine inducements in the form of more comfortable rolling stock or departure times closer to what the public required or sometimes provided faster trains to compen-

1899 Express trains: an international comparison

Country	Service	Mileage	Average mph of fastest train	3rd Class fare pence per mile
Britain	London-Milford	280	42	.90
France	Paris-Brest	381	30	No 3rd class
Germany	Berlin-Kiel	250	39	No 3rd class
Austria	Vienna-Trieste	373	29	.72

sate for their longer mileage. The GWR, nicknamed the 'Great Way Round', was in this situation between London and Exeter and London and Birmingham. Its London-Birmingham trains meandered through Didcot and Oxford covering a mileage of 130 miles, whereas the London & North Western Railway's trains ran in almost a straight line from Euston to Birmingham, covering a distance of only 113 miles. By the end of the century, by providing powerful locomotives to haul comparatively light trains, the best GWR train over this route took only seven minutes longer than the LNWR train. But this was a peak performance, and the GWR in due course decided to build itself a shorter London-Birmingham line.

In the last decade of the century, while many railways were achieving notable accelerations of their main-line passenger services, others were lagging behind. The Midland Railway was scathingly described as accelerating its London-Glasgow service at the average rate

BELOW: Great Western, a GWR record-breaker which averaged 55mph from London to Exeter in 1846. Originally a 2-2-2 with 8ft driving wheels, it later became a 4-2-2, with the addition of an extra front carrying axle.

ABOVE: *The GWR's 'Flying Dutchman' in 1887. This was a broad-gauge train, running on mixed-gauge track from London to Devon. The wide spacing of the cylinders, made possible by the broad gauge, is clearly visible.*

of six seconds per annum. The London, Brighton & South Coast's best London-Brighton train was scheduled at 46mph over the 50 miles, whereas the London & North Western at this time had a fish train which ran from Tebay to Preston (53 miles) at 47mph, prompting the comment that it was better to be a dead mackerel on the LNWR than a first-class passenger on the LBSCR.

But a few years later, the LBSCR proved that even a dead mackerel had to concede precedence to a dead queen, and it was characteristically perverse of that railway to produce its most exciting burst of speed in hauling a funeral train. Queen Victoria died on the Isle of Wight in 1901 and the LBSCR was entrusted with the funeral train from Portsmouth to London. Typically enough, the arrangements were muddled and the departure from Fareham was nine minutes behind schedule. The new King, who was due to meet the train in London, did not like being kept waiting, so the locomotivemen were advised to make the best speed they could. The result was that the late Queen, who in her lifetime had required the royal train to proceed at a safe and solemn pace, was hurtled to London at speeds in excess of 80mph.

The LBSCR, amid its general lethargy, by that time also managed to put on a London-Brighton service which covered the 51 miles in one hour exactly, but this ran only once a week. The LNWR, Britain's self-styled 'Premier Line', had done much better than that, and markedly improved its schedules in the 1890s. The best of its London-Holyhead trains by the end of the century averaged 50mph over the 264 miles, making only one stop *en route*, which was 10mph faster than in 1890. The Anglo-Scottish services, thanks to intense competition, were also much faster, with Glasgow eight hours from London, compared with nine hours in 1890. The GWR, which had been resting on its somewhat withered laurels for some decades, also stirred itself in the 1890s and accelerated many of its better trains. It ran a train over the 194 miles from London to Exeter at 50mph, and its best train to Bristol covered the 118 miles in 2¼ hours, an average of just over 52mph.

Between London and Bristol the GWR faced no competition, and a similar monopoly was enjoyed by the London & South Western with its London-Bournemouth services. The LSWR in 1899 introduced four new fast trains to Bournemouth, running non-stop over the 107 miles in 125 minutes. In these and a few other instances, improved schedules obviously were not stimulated by competition but simply, perhaps, by a quest for achievement and a wish to demonstrate the excellence of the company.

Some Victorian speed exploits

Year	Location	Mileage	Average mph	Locomotive	Railway
1847	Wolverton-Coventry	41	59	4-2-0	LNWR
1848	London-Didcot	53	67	4-2-2	GWR
1848	Derby-Altofts	64	56	2-2-2	MR
1888	Carlisle-Edinburgh	101	59	4-2-2	CR
1888	York-Newcastle	81	62	2-4-0	NER
1895	Crewe-Carlisle	141	67	2-4-0	LNWR
1896	London-Dover	78	57	4-4-0	LCDR

But the Midland Railway was running its best London-York train in 1899 on a schedule 9 minutes slower than a few years previously. Some other companies were equally retrograde, but it must be remembered that this last decade of the century was characterized by traffic growth and congestion, as well as by the running of heavier trains. Freight as well as passenger traffic was increasing, and on some trunk routes two tracks had become insufficient. The LNWR created a 4-track main line from London as far as Crewe, the GWR quadrupled from London to Didcot and then beyond, the Great Northern found it necessary to quadruple its line into London, and the London and South Western, because of increasing suburban traffic, quadrupled its main line from Waterloo in London as far as Basingstoke. In the last decade of the century the Midland, handling an enormous amount of coal traffic from the East Midlands, was quadrupling its line from that region as far as London, reserving two tracks for passenger and two for freight trains.

Passenger trains carried mail, parcels and passengers' baggage as well as people, and as traffic developed and stations became overloaded, longer stops were required. The introduction of dining cars enabled meal stops to be cut out and brought about fundamental changes in rolling stock design, resulting in fewer passengers per ton of train. Some railways, for a time, avoided this change in design by assuming that passengers wishing to eat *en route* would remain in the restaurant car throughout the journey, thus providing revenue seats to compensate for its weight, and denying access to the rest of the train from the dining car while the train was in motion. In due course, however, the side corridor and the concept of the restaurant car as a non-revenue service was accepted. The side corridor additionally provided toilets that would be accessible to all passengers, as for a short time they had been placed between two compartments, limiting access only from those two, a feature which could cause grave social embarrassment to the uninstructed traveller.

Possibly the Midland Railway's failure to accelerate its train services as fast as other companies was an indirect consequence of its provision of more comfortable trains. It had been the Midland which, in the 1870s, abolished the old third-class accommodation. It continued to sell third-class tickets which were valid on former second-class vehicles, as the old second-class classification had been abolished. This was a powerful encouragement for the poorer, but potentially numerous, class of passenger and led to a need for bigger trains. The Midland was also well to the fore in providing sleeping and dining accommodation along the longest of the competing routes between London and the north, trying to win custom by style and comfort. Gradually, other British companies imitated its two-class fare structure and experienced the same need to run heavier, more comfortable trains.

The other companies had resented the introduction of Pullman cars by the Midland, forecasting that the heavy weight of these vehicles, when included in a train of conventional stock, would turn them into juggernauts in the event of a collision. In fact, when heavier rolling stock was generally introduced in Britain, a number of companies stipulated that the new vehicles should not be included in trains of older stock, overlooking the point that the occupants of the heavy vehicles had an enhanced life expectancy in the event of an accident. This is not to say that any passenger rolling stock at this period was at

all safe by modern standards. The screw couplings were too weak to hold the vehicles in a line in a derailment, so the train would be scattered across the track or down an embankment. The prevalence of gas and oil illumination meant that disastrous fires could follow a mishap, and wooden bodies and frames provided little impact resistance. 'Telescoping', when the body of one coach would be forced into the body of the one in front of it, was the most dreaded consequence of a collision. Bad accidents, however, were rare, thanks to careful operating procedures. A feature of the American coaches imported by the Midland was their bogies. Instead of riding on four or six rigidly-held wheels, they rode on four-wheel swivelling trucks, or bogies, one at each end. The six-wheel swivelling truck, another American idea, also made a fleeting appearance on the Midland. In due course, seeing the need for more capacious vehicles, the other railways adopted the bogie coach, but by the end of the century these had appeared on only a few select trains. The majority of the better trains used six-wheelers,

while four-wheelers were used on secondary services. However these vehicles were neither comfortable at high speed, nor spacious, and were quickly dropped in the growing desire for faster schedules and a great deal more comfort.

Composite coaches, providing more than one class of accommodation in the same body, were very typical, and the final designs of composite six-wheelers showed considerable ingenuity in squeezing many functions into a body that was only about 30ft in length. The LNWR's design, for example, provided two third-class compartments, one second, and one first, with the first having access to a toilet compartment in the central and steadiest part of the vehicle. The second-class compartment, sometimes termed the 'honeymoon room', was in fact only half a compartment, or coupe. But in addition to this passenger space there was also a luggage compartment, which was an answer to the many problems caused by stowing baggage on the roof, as in stage-coach days, and which was becoming impracticable. This archaic practice had been one cause of the noise, fuss and general anarchy witnessed at the mainline stations, and was also the source of numerous complaints about lost luggage.

With the exception of a few newly-introduced trains of bogie stock, passenger trains were usually formed of a variety of unmatching vehicles, often of different age and usually of different profile; many railways at one period or other had favoured the clerestory roof, and this could be seen alongside eliptical roofs of varying radiuses. A typical train would have a brake van at both ends; each had a hand brake, provided accommodation for the guard, and had space for parcels, baggage, and perhaps mail. The passenger-carrying stock would be placed between these extremities, with proportions of first-, second- and third-class accommodation to meet the demands of that particular service. A few of the fastest trains did not accept third-class passengers, but this restriction was dying out in Britain, although it would survive in America and continental Europe.

The family saloon, a privately-hired coach, was very prominent in Britain. Outwardly it followed conventional form, being about 30ft long and 8ft wide (except on the GWR, where the recently-abolished broad gauge had left the useful legacy of wider clearances), its interior was designed for the use of a single family, typically for family holiday journeys. There was a central saloon, with longitudinal, softly upholstered seats. At one end there would be a smaller compartment for the servants, and at the other a luggage compartment. Such vehicles were in great demand on the lines to Scotland during the grouse season, but the coming of the sleeping car outmoded them in this service, whereupon some were converted to 'picnic saloons', designed for family outings.

Other vehicles which formed part of passenger trains were luggage vans, needed especially on holiday routes, for families would take a prodigious amount of

LEFT: *No.1, a Stirling outside-cylinder 'Single' of the Great Northern Railway, built in 1870 and now preserved in working order. This type was used in Anglo-Scottish and other services until superseded by 2-4-0 designs.*

BELOW: *One of the Midland Railway's classic inside-cylinder 'Singles'. This example was built in the Railway's Derby workshops in 1887 and is shown here at Bedford in Edwardian times.*

luggage with them, and also horseboxes. The latter, having the same wheels and underframes as passenger vehicles, provided a stall for one or two horses and a compartment for their attendant. 'Carriage trucks', which conveyed passengers' road carriages, were still to be seen although they were steadily disappearing.

Only a minority of long-distance trains had dining cars. The LNWR's first dining cars on trains to Liverpool and Manchester were of the early type built on a six-wheel underframe and could accommodate only 14 diners, who had to hold first-class tickets.

Bogie coaches, before the 1890s, had been adopted because they offered lower costs per seat-mile and also, as in the case of the LBSCR's businessman's express, to give a smoother ride. But now the best features of the different designs were combined to form what became the traditional British side-corridor train.

The Great Eastern Railway permitted second- and third-class passengers in its dining cars, and in the 1890s it built an all-class dining set of three non-bogie vehicles, making use of side corridors for access to the dining tables. In 1891 the GWR had introduced the first complete all-corridor, all-bogie, train. This was of only four vehicles, and the corridors were designed to give access to the separate men's and women's toilets. The gas-lit coaches were linked with bellows gangways, to be used only by the train guard, for this train had no dining car. It

went into service between London and Birkenhead in 1892, and received great public praise, even though gas was already being replaced by the more modern electric lighting. The GER and GWR concepts were subsequently combined in all-bogie, all-corridor trains in which passengers from any vehicle could walk to the dining car.

Another quite crucial step forward was the fitting of continuous automatic brakes to passenger trains. This was imposed by an Act of Parliament in 1889, although most railways had been moving in that direction for some years. 'Continuous' meant brakes acting together throughout the whole length of the trains, and 'automatic' in fact meant fail-safe. Some railways chose the Westinghouse compressed-air system, but the majority chose the vacuum brake. The co-existence of the two incompatible systems, as a result of Parliament not imposing a standard system, was a handicap which continued right into the period of the unified British Railways network. The new brakes not only made train travel safer, but also made high start-to-stop speeds more feasible as braking distances for stations and signals became shorter.

The average weight of express passenger trains probably rose from about 150 tons to over 200 tons, locomotive excluded, in the last decade of the nineteenth century. Train schedules had also become very demanding. Locomotive designers responded mainly by building

LEFT: *A 2-4-0 passenger engine of the Great Eastern Railway. Painted in the Company's Prussian-blue livery, these locomotives were a fine sight hauling trains in East Anglia around the turn of the century.*

BELOW: *One of the early 2-4-0 locomotives of the Midland Railway. This example was built in the 1860s. The 2-4-0 was a marked advance on the 'Single' but compared with its successor the 4-4-0 it was rough riding and harsh on the track at high speeds.*

ABOVE: *The 'Cauliflower' 0-6-0 of the LNWR was a simple and long-lived design. It was introduced in 1887, and examples survived into the 1950s. This picture shows one of the class in LMS days, when it was used for light freight services.*

RIGHT: *An 0-6-0 of the early twentieth century designed and built by the South Eastern & Chatham Railway at its Ashford works. Like many other examples of this wheel arrangement, this design had driving wheels of a little more than 5ft diameter, making it suitable for freight and secondary passenger trains.*

bigger machines, but were also beginning to turn their attention to new technologies in order to extract a great deal more power from a given amount of both coal and water.

The process of building ever-bigger varieties of what were still essentially Stephensonian locomotives had been continuing since the 1840s. In Britain, however, there had been an unusual addiction to the 'Single' for passenger work. This had a single driving axle and was therefore more free-running than a locomotive that had two sets of driving wheels joined by a heavy coupling rod. Most other countries had abandoned the Single, because its pair of driving wheels could only transmit a limited amount of power to the rails before wheel-slip set in. In Britain, where trains were light and gradients easy, these considerations were less pressing, and Singles were not only hauling fast trains in the 1890s, but were still being built by one company, the Midland Railway. In fact one of these MR Singles, *Princess of Wales*, built in 1900, won a Grand Prix at the Paris Exhibition of that year. Another classic Single type still at work was the Stirling Single of the Great Northern Railway. The Midland and GNR singles were of about the same size, but differed considerably in design. The GN used outside cylinders for easy access and cool environment whereas the MR preferred inside cylinders in the interest of steady running. As trains became heavier, the Singles on all railways were being replaced by locomotives with four coupled wheels. In fact, it was only the invention of steam sanding gear, which provided better adhesion between driving wheel and rail, that had given the Single concept a fresh lease of life in the late nineteenth century.

LEFT: *An 0-6-0 of Scotland's Caledonian Railway, now restored to its original blue livery, and photographed in a Highland setting even though the Caledonian was essentially a Lowland company.*

LEFT, BELOW: *Another restored Scottish 0-6-0, this example being a type used by the Caledonian's competitor, the North British Railway. Built in the late nineteenth century, several members of this class later received names to commemorate generals of the Great War. This locomotive is named Maude.*

LEFT: *An 0-6-0 of Scotland's Caledonian Railway, now restored to its original blue livery, and photographed in a Highland setting even though the Caledonian was essentially a Lowland company.*

LEFT, BELOW: *Another restored Scottish 0-6-0, this example being a type used by the Caledonian's competitor, the North British Railway. Built in the late nineteenth century, several members of this class later received names to commemorate generals of the Great War. This locomotive is named Maude.*

RIGHT, TOP: Cornubia, *one of the GWR's outside-framed 'Duke' class passenger 4-4-0s, introduced in 1895.*

RIGHT, LOWER: *An example of the GWR's fondness for its own past, this 4-4-0, shown hauling a light freight train on the four-track main line south of Didcot, belonged to a class almost identical with* Cornubia *illustrated above, but it was built in the late 1930s.*

Singles came in two-wheel arrangements. In the earlier decades the 2-2-2 was popular, the first '2' denoting a pair of small carrying wheels, the middle '2' indicating the driving wheels (which could be 8ft or more in diameter), and the final '2' denoting a pair of small carrying wheels under the firebox. Later, the leading pair of carrying wheels were replaced by a four-wheel bogie which increased stability at high speed, and it was as a 4-2-2 that the Single reached its apogee.

Heavier trains required more power than the light-footed Single could deliver, and the 2-4-0, with four coupled driving wheels, and a leading two-wheel truck to keep it steady, was developed. The Midland Railway had many examples of this locomotive, and so had the LNWR, whose 2-4-0 *Hardwicke* broke records in 1895.

The 2-4-0 engines of the Great Eastern Railway remained in service until the 1950s. The LBSCR reversed this wheel arrangement and its 'Gladstone' 0-4-2 type performed well with its London-Brighton trains.

Most of the big railways, and some of the smaller, used the 2-4-0, but the type never gained the popularity enjoyed by its successor, the 4-4-0. This wheel arrangement had long been used in America for both passenger and freight locomotives, but in Britain it was designed for passenger workings. It was bigger than the 2-4-0 and so could carry the larger boiler that sustained the required high horsepower. It came in many types. Dugald Drummond, locomotive superintendent of the North British and Caledonian railways in Scotland, and later of the London & South Western in England introduced designs which became a classic locomotive type. They were characterized by their simplicity and sturdiness, had inside cylinders and wheels of about 6ft 6in diameter. In contrast the 4-4-0 engines of the GWR had outside frames, an arrangement often used for inside-cylinder locomotives as the frames would prevent the stricken driving wheels flying off the engine in the event of a crank axle fracture. However, such accidents now happened rarely, but the GWR, not for the first or last time, was slow to change. Its 'Duke' class of 4-4-0 were of this type and had driving wheels of less than 6ft to fit them for the hilly Cornish lines.

Large driving wheels had always been preferred for the faster locomotives because they needed fewer revolutions per minute to maintain a given speed, and moving parts like pistons and balance weights moved more slowly. As lubricants improved and as locomotive design became more scientific, wheel diameter could be reduced from around 8ft to less than 7ft. A compromise was always being sought between the large wheel, admirable at the highest speeds, and the small wheel, not good for speed but excellent for tractive power. Locomotives designed primarily for freight work were sometimes used on secondary, slower, passenger services, but the true 'mixed traffic' locomotive, equally at home with freight or passenger, would only appear in the twentieth century.

LEFT: *One of the classic British 0-6-0 designs, the 'Dean Goods' of the GWR, shown here marshalling a train of inner-London suburban coaches. Despite its name, the class was frequently used on secondary passenger services. It was introduced in 1883 and examples were sent overseas in both world wars.*

BELOW: *Queen Empress, perhaps the most celebrated of the LNWR compound locomotives, on its way to be exhibited at the Chicago World Fair of 1893.*

It was noted by several observers that the performance of quite old locomotives seemed actually to improve with advancing age. The broad gauge Singles of the GWR, dating from mid-century but continuing to haul trains to the west until the final abolition of broad gauge in 1892, were a striking example of this. Some engineers explained this by the demand made on them towards the end of the century by train weights and schedules, but a later and more scientific explanation points to the substitution first of steel for iron rails, and then of improved and hardened steel for ordinary steel rail. Greater rigidity of the track meant that wheels depressed the rails less, and therefore vehicles rode more on top of the rail than in troughs caused by their own weight.

Most companies used old engines for branch lines and slow passenger trains that had been superseded on the mainline turns, whereas specific locomotive designs were being developed for freight. These locomotives had relatively small driving wheels of around 5ft diameter, and usually had a greater number of driving axles. The 0-6-0 became a favourite British wheel arrangement quite early in the railway age, but the larger 0-8-0 had appeared before the end of the century on certain lines handling heavy coal trains, and notably on the LNWR, which built hundreds of the type. The Midland Railway always seemed to use locomotives one size smaller than necessary and persisted in the use of its 0-6-0 for mineral traffic, often using two per train. Such doubleheading also represented a doubling of enginemen's wage costs, but labour, even skilled labour, was cheap in the Victorian economy, as was that other major railway requirement, coal. Cheap labour and cheap coal, and the absence of competition from other transport modes were perhaps the essential elements that shaped the Victorian railway scene.

ABOVE: *An LNWR 0-6-0, built in 1862 at the Company's Crewe works. Like its descendant, the 'Cauliflower' type, this design exemplifies LNWR locomotive practice with its emphasis on simplicity and ruggedness, and its lack of refinement.*

RIGHT: *A London Chatham & Dover Railway 0-6-0, built in 1873 and intended mainly for freight service.*

THE RACE TO THE NORTH

LEFT: *The southbound '2 pm Corridor' about to leave Glasgow around 1908. The resplendent 4-6-0 is* Cardean, *a frequent and celebrated performer on this service. In the other platform a local train is waiting to leave, hauled by an equally spotless, but older, 2-4-0 locomotive.*

Railway traffic is most profitable over the longest distances, which is why British railway companies put so much of their effort into developing their longer routes, thus attracting passengers and freight which had hitherto travelled over other companies' lines. Although the various declared and undeclared railway 'races' had a sporting element, their underlying motive was inevitably commercial, driven by the quest for higher profits obtainable from a greater share of the traffic, or the creation of a reputation that would encourage shippers and passengers to use a particular railway in future.

The longest mainline hauls were from southern England to Scotland, and so the London to Scotland services were affected by strong competitive influences right up to the nationalisation of railways in 1948.

Until the British railway amalgamation of 1923, when the various companies were merged into four large companies, the competing routes from London to Scotland were formed by consortia of companies making end-on links. Thus, the West Coast Route was formed by the LNWR, whose main line left its Euston terminal in London and went via the LNWR's own railway town of Crewe over the hills of Westmoreland to Carlisle, where Scotland's Caledonian Railway took over the trains for their continuation to Glasgow, Edinburgh, Perth and Aberdeen. The competing East Coast Route left Kings Cross Station in London as the Great Northern Railway, linked with the North Eastern Railway at York, and then in Scotland continued over the North British Railway. Later, a third viable consortium was formed by the Midland Railway and its Scottish associates, but this could not compete in terms of speed, only in terms of comfort and style.

In Victorian times, the top trains of the West and East coast routes were, respectively, the 10am from Euston (the future 'Royal Scot'), and the 10am from Kings Cross (the future 'Flying Scotsman', at the time known as the 'Special Scotch Express'). The latter train took nine hours to reach Edinburgh, while the West Coast rival took ten. The West Coast, although a more hilly and longer route, had the compensation of a shorter route to Glasgow. Moreover, its trains ran well-filled because it accepted third-class passengers, unlike the East Coast's 'Special Scotch Express'.

In late 1887, the East Coast train did begin to convey third-class passengers, and this had an immediate effect on the loading of the 10am from Euston. The West Coast consortium thereupon decided it had to equal the nine-hour schedule of its competitor, and there began a succession of schedule cuts as each consortium strove to bring its time below that of its competitor. This, in essence, was the 1888 'Race to the North' which brought the London-Edinburgh schedule of both trains down to eight hours by August 1888, when a truce was reached. This represented fast running, especially over the West Coast route, which, at 400 miles, was seven miles longer than the East Coast route and included a 20-minute meal stop at Preston. For both of the competitors the eight-hour schedule meant an average speed, including stops, of almost 50mph.

The next race to the north broke out in 1895, and seems to have resulted from a premeditated act of aggression by the West Coast companies. This race involved the night expresses from London to Aberdeen, and for some weeks the East Coast managements were not aware that in fact a race was in progress. The West

Coast service was officially accelerated by 40 minutes, but was operated in a helter-skelter fashion with no adherence to timetables. Between stops, the train ran as fast as possible, and at stops was signalled away as soon as it was ready, without waiting for the official departure time. The best run that summer by the West Coast service was in a time of 512 minutes for the 540 miles, an average of 63mph. The East Coast train, the future 'Aberdonian', was also accelerated but observed intermediate departure times quite scrupulously, although its official schedule was changed on almost a daily basis. Its best run was 520 minutes for the 524 miles.

In terms of the quickest run, the West Coast won, but for both consortia, and for British railways in general, the race was good publicity. It attracted intense interest from the press and public, including an interest in train speeds, which lasted for decades and was equally fascinating for those of sporting or technical bent.

In retrospect, a more searching look at the 1888 and 1895 races raises the question of whether the passengers benefited; the answer is probably not at all. This was a foretaste of the twentieth century's 'improvement

ABOVE: *The role of the railways in integrating Scotland and Wales into the United Kingdom was so unquestioned that a* Punch *cartoon of 1945 could raise a laugh by presenting an alternative situation.*

BELOW: Hardwicke, *the LNWR 2-4-0 which broke records in the 1895 race to the North.*

1895 Race to the North: Fastest sectional averages

Section	Railway	Locomotive	Mileage	mph
Crewe-Carlisle	LNWR	2-4-0 *Hardwicke*	141	67
Perth-Aberdeen	CR	4-4-0 No 17	90	67
Newcastle-Edinburgh	NER	4-4-0 No 1620	124	66
Grantham-York	GNR	4-2-2 No 775	83	65

ABOVE: *The '2 pm Corridor' of the LNWR in 1913, on its way from London Euston to Glasgow. The locomotive is one of the LNWR's last passenger designs, the 'Claughton' class 4-6-0.*

that worsens'. To arrive at Aberdeen at 6am was not a heavenly novelty, especially after a night spent hurtling over curves and crossings at excessive speeds. In the 1888 race, West Coast passengers were given only 20 minutes to eat their meal at Preston, again not a life-enhancing experience. Lastly, although the eye-witness report that one of the locomotives in the races rounded a curve with its offside wheels out of touch with the rail was uncorroborated, there is no doubt that speed restrictions were violated and that it was only luck which saved the trains from lethal mishap.

This kind of race to the north was not repeated after 1895, and at the turn of the century the consortia reached an agreement implying that no day train would be scheduled at less than 8¼ hours between London and Edinburgh or London and Glasgow, but efforts to compete by means of exceptionally attractive trains continued.

The situation was not changed by the entry of a third competitor, the Midland Railway and its Scottish ally the Glasgow & South Western. In the mid-1870s, the MR had built a main line out of Leeds to Carlisle, which included the awesome Settle & Carlisle line. This line crossed and recrossed the fells of northern England by a series of tunnels and viaducts, and, at Ais Gill, reached the highest point (1169ft) of any British main line. The difficult terrain, and the longer mileage, put any competitive scheduling out of the question, but a growing number of passengers accepted the slower transit because the MR's bogie coaches were far more comfortable than

the bumpy six-wheelers then offered by the other two routes. The MR also operated Pullman vehicles. Its best Anglo-Scottish express, known as the 'Scotchman' in England, was called the 'Pullman' in Scotland. In 1888, while the two other companies were indulging in their racing activities, the MR ran the 'Scotchman' as two trains, one to Glasgow and the other to Edinburgh, using the North British Railway's line between Carlisle and Edinburgh.

In later years the MR tried hard to keep its share of the market. What was later the 'Thames-Forth Express' from London to Edinburgh ran non-stop in the summer as far as Leeds (196 miles); and the MR's summer night express, from its magnificent St Pancras terminus in London to the Scottish Highlands, carried through sleeping cars and through coaches to both sides of Scotland and the centre as well, via Fort William, Aberdeen, Inverness, and Perth. With Glasgow 424 miles from London by the MR against 401 miles by the West Coast route, this consortium did well to reduce its London-Glasgow time to 8¾ hours.

The West Coast consortium, competing as much with the Midland as with the East Coast Route, introduced its '2pm Corridor'. This was a completely new train for the afternoon Anglo-Scottish service. At the turn of the century, it was normally a 10-car formation, six vehicles being destined for Glasgow with another two for Aberdeen, and two more for Edinburgh. By this time the LNWR had decided to provide dining accommodation for both first and third classes, so half of the Glasgow section, situated immediately behind the locomotive, was devoted to eating. The composition of this Glasgow section, from front to rear, was combined brakevan and third-class car, a corridor third, a third diner, a first-class diner with kitchen, a first dining car, and a corridor first. The Edinburgh and Aberdeen sections were identical, each consisting of a first/third composite and a third/brake. The new rolling stock for this train was wider than previous coaches and the cars were 45ft long. The first-class coaches were particularly luxurious, with compartments designed to seat only four passengers.

In the decade preceding World War I, the 'Corridor' was one of the finest British trains. The coaches were painted in a purplish-brown and white livery, and looked magnificent whether running behind a glossy black LNWR locomotive in England or a blue Caledonian Railway locomotive in Scotland. The train was given even better rolling stock in 1908, and with the exception of the dining cars ran on 6-wheel bogies. The 2pm departure remained, and the train called only at Willesden, Rugby, Crewe, Preston, and Carlisle, although a stop was necessary at Beattock, north of Carlisle, to attach a pusher engine for Beattock Bank, and also at Carstairs, to detach the Edinburgh section. Arrival at Glasgow was at 10.20pm and at Edinburgh at 10.30pm. The southbound train, which picked up the Edinburgh coaches at Preston, made its longest non-stop run over the 102 miles between Glasgow and Carlisle, and by 1914, with more powerful locomotives available, the 'Corridor' became as heavy as 400 tons south of Preston. However during the War, it lost its dining cars, was given a longer schedule, and for a time was the only West Coast day service to Scotland.

With so much pride and capital lavished on the 'Corridor', it is not surprising that the long-established 10am from Euston was allowed to fall into second place. Until its temporary disappearance during World War I, it left

London with its Edinburgh and Glasgow sections combined, although at Crewe these sections, having picked up Birmingham-Edinburgh and Birmingham-Glasgow coaches, proceeded north separately. However on the south-bound trip, the Glasgow section was subjected to flagging-down at Motherwell by any passenger on that station wishing to use it, a remarkable occurrence for a top-class express.

The East Coast's 10am departure from London continued to be its most prestigious train known, unofficially, as the 'Flying Scotsman'. By agreement with the West Coast service, its London-Edinburgh schedule was kept at 8¼ hours, once the 15-minute lunch break at York was abolished in 1900. The change coincided with the incorporation of dining cars in the train, which were provided along with completely new rolling stock in that year. The normal formation was henceforward eight 65ft cars of a design quite novel for Britain. They had Pullman vestibules at each end and buckeye automatic couplers; an increased safety factor in accidents. The train weighed 265 tons and, like most other fast trains, did not give a very high seat-per-ton ratio, carying only 50 first- and 211 third-class passengers. These trains were replaced in 1914; the new formations were heavier and included three restaurant cars, one of which was entirely devoted to kitchen and pantry space. During the War, these dining cars were removed to provide extra seating, and the schedule was lengthened to almost ten hours.

The agreement to maintain 8¼-hour schedules applied only to day trains, so the East Coast's fastest Anglo-Scottish train was its Highland sleeper, which later became the 'Aberdonian'. This managed the London-Edinburgh sector in 7¾ hours even though it was quite a heavy train.

For the Anglo-Scottish passenger, there was a variety of routes and trains from which to choose. Surprisingly, many regular passengers had no wish to exploit this variety of style and scenery, but travelled consistently with the same consortium. When people had strong convictions as to which was the 'best' railway company, to travel by another seemed quite disloyal.

BELOW: *One of the large Atlantic locomotives hard at work on the Great Northern main line in 1904. The 'somersault' form of signal arm, seen here, was characteristic of the GNR.*

RIGHT: *One of the earlier, smaller, Great Northern Atlantics poses for pictures a few weeks after construction in 1900, together with a new train of 12-wheelers.*

The companies which made up the consortia also ran their own services to other northern cities, sometimes competitively and sometimes not. Services from Liverpool and Manchester to London were, strictly speaking, competitive, because there were alternative companies and routes, but in both cases the LNWR had the lion's share of the traffic because its lines were better placed to provide these services. In 1905, it introduced the best train to Liverpool, the future 'Merseyside Express', leaving London at 5.55pm and running non-stop as far as the Liverpool suburbs. The Great Northern and Great Central could hardly match it, still less the GWR, whose trains were merely continuations of its Birmingham expresses, taken northwards as far as Chester, then reversed and hauled not to Liverpool but to Birkenhead, where the passenger was expected to embark on a ferry for the final minutes of the journey.

To Manchester the evening LNWR train from London, later named the 'Lancastrian', ran non-stop to Stockport (183 miles) and brought Manchester to within 3½ hours of the capital. Three other railways provided a London-Manchester service, but could not quite match those timings. The MR managed a 3-hour 40-minute schedule by 1914, while the Great Northern could offer only 4¼ hours and the new Great Central 5½ hours. Probably customer loyalty was less important than traffic from intermediate stations in filling the GN and GC trains, although the GC was already rivalling the Midland in its provision of luxurious passenger accommodation. But on the whole, the LNWR did not need to try very hard to maintain its supremacy.

On the other side of the country, the Great Northern and North Eastern railways were co-operating in the London-Newcastle traffic, and with their virtual monopoly did not need to run to especially fast schedules. On the other hand they did not dawdle either, and throughout Britain in this pre-1914 decade there were routes, not subject to competition, but nevertheless provided with creditably timed trains. Public opinion was presumably an important factor here, as a railway needed a reputation for smartness in the passenger field to encourage shippers to use it for their freight. Freight brought in more money than passengers, and undoubtedly there were fast passenger trains which in more modern times would have been described as 'loss-leaders'. But railway

LEFT: *The celebrated LNWR compound* Jeanie Deans, *which for years hauled the West Coast 'Corridor'. On one occasion it hauled a 350-ton load between Nuneaton and Willesden (92 miles) at an average of 54mph.*

ABOVE: *The restored Midland Railway compound No.1000 heads a present-day excursion train. These 4-4-0 engines were the most successful of the British compounds and were built over almost three decades. No.1000 had a smaller boiler when originally built in 1902.*

accounting procedures were inefficient and it proved very difficult to establish which trains were profitable, and which were not. Establishing costs per passenger-mile was subject to so many assumptions it was practically worthless, so the rule of thumb, 'the more passengers the better', was more or less accepted.

The last pre-1914 years witnessed the establishment of the all-bogie, all-corridor train as Britain's main-line standard. On the main lines to the north, with their intense competition and their long distances, passenger comfort had high priority, and a number of coach designs were developed especially for this traffic. East Coast Joint Stock (the name given to coaches designed for the East Coast Route, and equipped with two brake systems), was distinguished by features that had economic advantages but also contributed to safety. Among these were buckeye couplers, substitution of electric lighting for gas, and the use of steel underframes in place of the previous construction making use of wooden sole-bars reinforced by iron trusses. The kitchen cars introduced for the 'Flying Scotsman', in 1914, were of steel construction, although this rolling stock provided little extra comfort than the original bogie stock.

The choice between vestibule and side-door design had still not been settled. Although the East and West coast trains featured vestibule stock (that is, having the doors leading off a vestibule at each end of the vehicle), the MR preferred side doors for each compartment. Midland trains, both on this route and elsewhere, were said to be the grandest in the country, being painted, engine and coaches alike, in a bright maroon paint known officially as crimson lake, and lettered in gilt. Inside, the upholstery varied but was usually magnificent, even the third class featuring gold and purple arabesque, while

grass-green velvet could be found in the first class. But in its persistence with gas lighting long after electricity had proved itself, the MR was retrograde, and it took two passenger train collisions and the ensuing fires, to change this. These fires, disastrous in themselves, had been rendered more terrible by the MR's additional practice of fixing metal bars over its windows.

The West Coast Joint Stock was of LNWR design, and based on 12-wheel designs already used for the Liverpool boat trains. These were vestibuled, but for the Anglo-Scottish trains different interiors were used. The coaches were now 9ft wide and 65ft long, and weighed as much as 40 tons, because of the heavier but easier riding 6-wheel bogies. More or less standard LNWR furnishing was used, with figured green Blenheim moquette for the first class seats, and crimson and black striped plush for the third class. The provision of filtered drinking water was provided in the coaches, a highly unusual practice for Britain, which remained so. Electric lighting was used, and the window blinds were supplemented by curtains that could be drawn across the full width of the windows. The heavy bogies combined with the superb LNWR track made these trains exceptionally smooth-riding and they remained popular for years, and it was not until the late 1920s that new coaches were again introduced for this train service.

In a sense, these West Coast vehicles were too good, and for its other express trains the LNWR used somewhat less luxurious 8-wheeled stock; 57ft vehicles with, usually, high elliptical roofs, and side doors in preference to vestibules.

Whereas specially designed trains were built for the Anglo-Scottish services, specially designed locomotives were not built, although there were several cases when

RIGHT: *Boiler washout for one of the Midland compounds in 1911. Clearing boilers of sludge deposited by the water was a frequent, typically weekly, job.*

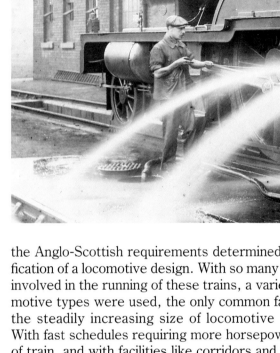

RIGHT: *Boiler washout for one of the Midland compounds in 1911. Clearing boilers of sludge deposited by the water was a frequent, typically weekly, job.*

ABOVE: *Caledonian Railway No. 123, a massive 'Single' built in 1886 and a distinguished participant in the 1888 race to the North.*

the Anglo-Scottish requirements determined the specification of a locomotive design. With so many companies involved in the running of these trains, a variety of locomotive types were used, the only common factor being the steadily increasing size of locomotive employed. With fast schedules requiring more horsepower per ton of train, and with facilities like corridors and dining cars reducing the number of passengers per ton, bigger locomotives or more numerous trains were the only solutions, and more numerous trains presented grave operating difficulties as well as raising costs per passenger.

Taking the railways in turn, the LNWR was perhaps the most interesting from the locomotive point of view. In the 1895 race to Aberdeen, it had used its 2-4-0 'Precedent' type almost exclusively and one of them, *Hardwicke*, had achieved the fastest of all the runs, hauling a light 72-ton train over the hilly section from Crewe to Carlisle at an average of 67mph. The 'Precedents' were simple engines, which stood up well to hard treatment, but were too small for the heavier trains of later years, and so they were replaced by various types of more complex locomotives. The latter were compound locomotives, engines which used their steam twice in successive cylinders, and were not altogether successful on the LNWR. However, one of them, *Jeanie Deans*, worked the '2pm Corridor' to Crewe and back every day, year after year, accumulating very creditable annual mileages in the process. On the whole the compounds were disappointing, and it became customary to entrust the heavier trains to two locomotives.

But in 1904, following a change of locomotive superintendent, there was a reversion to conventional, simple, designs in the 'Precursor' class of 4-4-0. Like the 'Precedents', of which they could perhaps be regarded as

an enlarged version, the 'Precursors' could be worked hard and, indeed, their sustained power output was limited as much by the endurance of the fireman as by their boiler dimensions. The later 'George the Fifth' class was very similar, but incorporated steam superheaters for greater efficiency, and it was not long before the 'Precursors' were rebuilt to the same standard. Between London and Crewe, these engines regularly hauled 400-ton trains and reached speeds of around 70mph at some points of the trip. Bigger, 4-6-0, versions of these engines, the 'Prince of Wales' and the 'Experiment' classes, were used north of Crewe, where greater tractive power was needed for the hills of Westmoreland, and particularly the arduous climb of Shap Fell. One of the 'Experiments' was timed at 93mph, while descending a gradient between Penrith and Carlisle.

On the eve of World War I, the LNWR introduced the 'Claughton' 4-6-0, with four cylinders instead of the two of its predecessors. These engines were used for the southern sector of the run, but their performance was little better than those of the 4-4-0s.

The Midland Railway, although long devoted to the Single, at the turn of the century did build 4-4-0 engines for its heavier trains. It was notable, too, for the 'Midland Compounds', compound 4-4-0s that were much more successful than the compounds of the LNWR. On the Settle & Carlisle section especially, where sustained high output was required, the compounds operated at considerable savings of coal and water. They were so competent that the MR did not progress to larger 4-6-0 designs.

The LNWR's partner, the Caledonian Railway, was very different in its locomotive policy. In the 1888 race, it used a Single locomotive for the West Coast train north

of Carlisle. However, this Single, the unique No 123, was as big as a 4-4-0, and performed accordingly. By the time of the 1895 race, the CR was using 4-4-0 locomotives, mainly designed by Dugald Drummond, of a classic simplicity. Some later locomotives also took part, including the famous 'Dunlastair' type, in which boiler dimensions were quite large for that period. Indeed, in succeeding years the Caledonian had a 'big boiler' policy, and the Caledonian 4-4-0s certainly had good steam-raising capacity, too.

By 1914, the CR had introduced enlarged versions of its successful 4-4-0 in the form of the 4-6-0, the extra driving axle enabling extra power to be transmitted and an even bigger boiler to be carried. One of these 4-6-0s, *Cardean*, was for years reserved for the Scottish haulage of the '2pm Corridor'. It had been hoped that *Cardean*'s higher horsepower would make a banker superfluous up the Beattock incline, but this hope was disappointed. With the need to haul 300-ton trains up the 1 in 75 gradient at over 25mph, a considerably larger engine would have been required. But *Cardean*, wearing her Caledonian blue livery and sounding her deep Caledonian siren, was one of the best-known locomotives of that time in Britain.

It was on the East Coast route that the most striking advances in locomotive design were made, although at first this was not apparent. In the 1895 race to Aberdeen, the Great Northern had used Stirling Singles for its part of the run, although the North Eastern was able to muster some of its large 4-4-0 types, one of which covered the Newcastle-Edinburgh sector at an average of 66mph with a 100-ton train. The North British Railway had contributed its rather lean 4-4-0s, which put up a performance surprising for their limited size and traditional design. However, after that year the GNR progressed to some rather undistinguished 4-4-0 types before changing to the 4-4-2, a novelty for Britain. The 4-4-2, or Atlantic, was regarded as more free-running than the 4-6-0 and, although more liable to slip, had the advantage that a larger firebox could be accommodated. The first GNR Atlantics were good but not outstanding locomotives. They put up some creditable performances with the 'Special Scotch Express', but were soon succeeded by a larger 4-4-2 which, when later enhanced by superheating, achieved startling performances. This type proved to be so good that some were also built for the London Brighton & South Coast Railway. Finally, just as it was about to disappear with the Railway Amalgamation, the

ABOVE: *No.17, a Caledonian Railway 4-4-0 built in the Dugald Drummond tradition.*

RIGHT, TOP: Henry Oakley , *the preserved example of the smaller Great Northern Atlantic.*

RIGHT: *Another view of Henry Oakley, at work on the Keighley & Worth Valley Railway. The first of the class to be built, in 1898, this locomotive was also the first British 4-4-2, a wheel arrangement that never became very popular.*

GNR produced yet another enlargement, this time a 4-6-2, or Pacific, designed by Nigel Gresley and the forerunner of the high-speed, high-power, locomotives of the 1930s.

In 1914, this most fascinating period of the age of steam came to an end in Britain. During World War I the railways were obliged to put aside their more sophisticated services – their fastest trains, their dining cars, their grouse specials – in aid of the war effort. Schedules were lengthened, while train lengths grew. However, there was one record-breaking run in 1916.

Lord Kitchener was despatched in a special train from Kings Cross to Scotland on the first stage of a mission to Russia. Half an hour after his train had left, a Foreign Office representative arrived at Kings Cross with documents, and requested a special train to catch up with Kitchener's. Within half an hour a large Atlantic was marshalled with two coaches, and this big engine and light train averaged 70mph over 58 miles between Hatfield and Peterborough. The train caught up with Kitchener's special at York; at an average speed of 66mph it beat the 1895 London-Doncaster record by two minutes. Kitchener then proceeded to his cruiser, in which he was drowned only a few days later.

SPEED
TO THE
WEST

LEFT: *A 'King' class engine
with a London-Birkenhead
train topping Hatton Bank.*

Another long-distance competitive route was from London to the southwest, dominated by the Great Western Railway, which also had a virtual monopoly to South Wales, Bristol, and across the Cotswolds. Unlike the routes to the north, the GWR and London & South Western Railway trains to Plymouth and Exeter did not link great industrial and population centres, but derived much traffic from the intermediate stations.

The GWR's route was formed by its original well-engineered route from London to Bristol making an end-on connection with its allied railway, the Bristol & Exeter, which in turn connected with lines built by the South Devon Railway. These two railways had soon been absorbed by the GWR. It was a somewhat roundabout route, and on the map looked much less direct than the LSWR's main line through Salisbury. In fact the GWR London-Exeter route was 194 miles, compared to the LSWR's 172 miles. Both lines took a devious route in order to avoid the worst of Dartmoor. To the west of Exeter, the GWR curved round to the south, close to the coast, and the LSWR took a circular northern alignment. With some exceptions, the two companies' branch lines in the west were arranged accordingly, with North Cornwall in particular being the preserve of the LSWR while the GWR had its south Devon branches. These branches offered both companies the development of seaside resorts that generated long-distance traffic in the holiday season.

The GWR's 'Cornishman' was one of the best-known trains to the southwest. Like many named trains at the time, its title was quite unofficial, marked neither on the train itself nor in the timetables. There is a well-known picture of this train leaving Paddington in London on 20 May 1892, as the last broad-gauge train to leave for Cornwall before the change from 7ft to 4ft 8½in gauge. It had made its maiden run in 1890 and in its first years had been a broad-gauge express, hauled by Single locomotives of 1850s' vintage. At that time it was not only the

GWR Twentieth-century passenger locomotive development

Type	Year	Wheel arrangement	Cylinders (ins)	Coupled wheel diameter	Grate area (Sq ft)	Boiler pressure psi	Tractive effort (lbs)	Weight on coupled (tons)
City	1903	4-4-0	18×26	6ft 8in	21	195	17,800	37
Saint	1905	4-6-0	18×30	6ft 8in	27	225	24,400	55
Star	1907	4-6-0	(4) 15×26	6ft 8in	27	225	27,800	55
Castle	1923	4-6-0	(4) 16×26	6ft 8in	29	225	31,600	59
King	1927	4-6-0	(4) 16×28	6ft 6in	34	250	40,300	67

(In this and other tables, dimensions are to the nearest inch, foot, pound and ton)

ABOVE: *The 'Cornish Riviera Limited', equipped with wide-body coaches, about to leave London Paddington in 1929.*

LEFT: *A GWR 'Star' (right) meets a 'Castle' near Exeter.*

RIGHT, TOP: *The GWR timetable map of 1911, mischievously implying that the Company not only served all of England and Wales, but also Scotland, Ireland and northern France.*

RIGHT, BOTTOM: *The 'Cornish Riviera' leaves Penzance in 1954.*

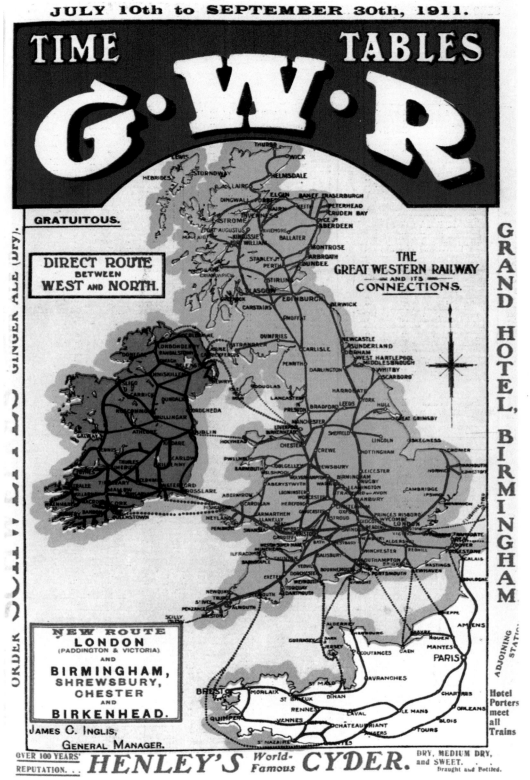

Fastest GWR schedules: London to Exeter

Year	Miles	Time	Average mph
1888	194 (via Bristol)	4h 15m	46
1899	194 (via Bristol)	3h 43m	52
1912	174 (via Westbury)	3h 0m	58
1924	174 (via Westbury)	3h 0m	58
1939	174 (via Westbury)	2h 49m	62
1951	174 (via Westbury)	3h 3m	57

fastest train to the west but also one of the fastest in Britain. It was quickest in the eastbound direction, leaving the GWR's western outpost of Penzance at 11.15am and arriving in Paddington at 7.50pm, taking 8 hours 35 minutes for the 325 miles. This timing included the compulsory refreshment stop at Swindon, but in 1895 the GWR paid the caterers the huge sum of £100,000 to buy out of the old contract which enforced these obligatory meal stops. From this Swindon stop, the 'Cornishman' was timed to run to Paddington at a 53mph average. Already, the superbly engineered Swindon-Paddington section, which sloped very gently downwards towards London, was something of a GWR racetrack.

Water troughs, long pans placed between the rails from which water could be scooped up by a locomotive at speed, had been invented by the LNWR and were soon imitated by other railways. At the same time as the abolition of the compulsory Swindon stop, the GWR laid down its own water troughs at Goring, near Reading, and Keynsham, near Bath. Non-stop running thereupon became possible between London and Bristol. By 1903, the 'Cornishman' had brought the London-Bristol time down to 2 hours for the 118 miles, an average speed of 59mph.

In the summer season the train ran in two parts, and the relief part, intended for passengers to Cornwall, ran from Paddington to Exeter. This part consisted of only five bogie coaches but, at 194 miles, covered at almost 52mph, this was the world's longest non-stop run. However, suddenly, despite its fame, the 'Cornishman' was allowed to disappear. In 1904 it was replaced by the new 'Cornish Riviera Express' and the title was forgotten, although it was revived in the 1950s for a train from Wolverhampton to Penzance.

The 'Cornish Riviera Express' ran non-stop as far as Plymouth, a distance of 246 miles, which became the new longest non-stop run. The train still lacked an official name, and its rolling stock, although of high standard, was like that of other GWR expresses. It consisted of six bogie coaches with clerestory roofs, together with a more modern, 68ft elliptical-roofed dining car, making a trailing load of about 200 tons.

In 1906, the GWR completed a cut-off route, so that trains to the west could continue past Reading, via Westbury, to rejoin the old main line at Taunton. This cut out the circuitous line through Swindon and Bristol and reduced the distance to Plymouth by 20 miles. The rival LSWR had little chance now of competing on this route for the traffic from London to Plymouth and

LEFT: *The cover of the thick 1938* Holiday Haunts, *obtainable at all GWR stations for just sixpence.*

ABOVE: *The GWR was a pioneer user of the motor omnibus, and not just for advertising, as shown here.*

ABOVE: *An alluring GWR holiday poster.*

RIGHT: *'West Country' Pacifics at work on the Ilfracombe line, a former outpost of the LSWR.*

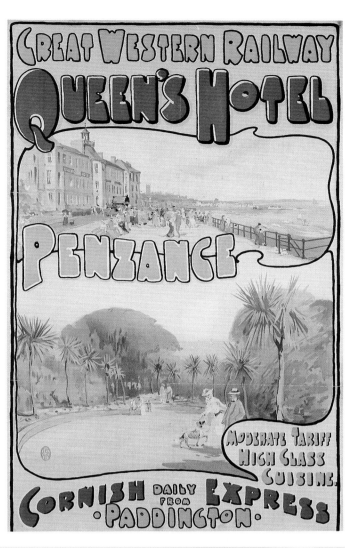

RIGHT: *The GWR, like other railway companies, operated its own hotels, including this one at Penzance.*

Exeter, although its trains were always much used by passengers bound for LSWR branch lines in Devon and Cornwall.

The new route coincided with a move to a 10.30am departure time for the 'Cornish Riviera Express', and this remained fixed for the rest of the steam age. Arrival at Penzance was at 5.05pm, despite quite a number of stops inside Cornwall. For this train, the GWR introduced some coaches that, at 70ft long, were the biggest eight-wheelers so far seen in Britain. They were notable, too, in that their end doors were recessed. The new GWR breed of 4-6-0 locomotives was being introduced on this train, replacing the outside-framed 'City' class 4-4-0 locomotives previously used. GWR locomotive policy, so far as passenger engines were concerned, was strongly influenced by the needs of the main line to Plymouth and in particular by the stiff gradients in South Devon, where Dainton Bank and Hemerdon Bank, steep winding inclines, provided some of the most arduous locomotive duties in Britain. Dainton included a stretch at 1 in 36, an inclination unsurpassed on any other British main line, while Hemerdon presented London-bound trains leaving Plymouth with a gruelling 2¼ miles at 1 in 42.

The 'Cornish Riviera Limited', as it was by then officially titled, made great use of slip coaches, as did the GWR in general. These were coaches with a special coupling and control post which could be detached from the rear of a train in motion. An extra guard operated the slip mechanism at the moment when, taking into consideration train speed and weather, the slipped coach had

enough momentum to take it into the platform of the intermediate station which the main part of the train had just passed through. Thus a non-stop train could actually carry passengers for intermediate stations, as long as they sat in the coach reserved for them. The 'Cornish Riviera Limited' slipped successive coaches for Westbury, Taunton and Exeter as it dashed to its first stop at Plymouth. On this particular train, the slip coaches also had the useful effect of progressively reducing the load as the gradients became more severe.

By World War II, the Exeter slip had been replaced by a regular stop at that city, in order to take on passengers travelling from Exeter further west. The Taunton and Westbury slips had both grown to two coaches where the former was taken onward to serve Ilfracombe and Minehead, and the latter to Weymouth. In addition, the main train detached coaches at various junctions for working over the branch lines. The St Ives coach was dropped at St Erth, the coach for Falmouth at Truro, the Newquay coach at Par, and the coach for Kingsbridge at Exeter. All these destinations were holiday resorts which had been developed by the presence of the railway and by a continuous advertising campaign, often run in co-operation with a resort's town council.

The GWR was not, of course, the only railway to advertise the virtues of spending holidays at resorts on its own system, nor was it the only one to take active steps in making these resorts more attractive by, for example, building its own superior hotels. But it was certainly a pace-setter in this regard. Its posters, which advertised specific resorts and which often featured a picture of one of its trains 'speeding to the west', were displayed prominently on its stations. It organised numerous excursion trains to the resorts, and it published useful tourist material, such as its annual *Holiday Haunts*, a massive volume, costing only sixpence, which served both as a guide book to places on the GWR and as a hotel and boarding house listing. In this endeavour the GWR, like the other British railways, had a great success and its efforts coincided with the emergence of a broad social class that could afford to spend annual holidays at the seaside.

The surge in holiday traffic was so great in the twentieth century and trains were so much faster, that many people were prepared to travel great distances to reach the resort of their choice. Trains started to run from one railway to another, connecting an industrial or populous area to a coastal resort. Typical of these was the Bradford to Paignton service, which was later titled the 'Devonian', a result of co-operation between the Midland and GW railways. The 'Sunny South Express', perhaps the best-known holiday train, did not touch the GWR. It ran from Manchester to Brighton as a joint venture of the LNWR and LBSCR, which began in 1904 and quickly prospered. At one period, it was hauled by an LBSCR locomotive over the LNWR between Rugby and Brighton.

After World War I, the 'Cornish Riviera Limited' grew as it became more popular; 70ft flush-sided coaches replaced the original stock, to be in their turn replaced by another new set of coaches and then, on the eve of World War II, by luxurious extra-wide coaches. The restaurant car grew to a three-car set: kitchen car, first-class car, third-class car. The train formation was typically 14 vehicles, making a load of more than 500 tons. As it grew, bigger engines were allocated to it. The 4-cylinder 'Stars' of pre-war days were replaced from

1923 by the similar but larger 'Castles', and then by the final enlargement of the type, the 'Kings'. 'Castles' continued to be used beyond Plymouth, however, as the 'Kings' were too heavy for the Saltash Bridge, west of Plymouth. By 1939, the average speed from London to the first stop at Exeter was almost 62mph.

The LSWR's main train to the west used to leave Waterloo Station in London about half an hour after the 'Cornish Riviera Limited' left Paddington. In 1926, after the line had become part of the new Southern Railway, the title of 'Atlantic Coast Express' was bestowed on this train, a name which perfectly represented its purpose, for it was designed less to serve Exeter and Plymouth than those coastal resorts at the end of Southern Railway branch lines in Devon and Cornwall. In its final years, it exceeded all other British trains in the number of separate sections it included. From the locomotive end it typically comprised three coaches for Ilfracombe, then individual coaches for Torrington, Padstow, Bude and Plymouth. The three-vehicle dining car set came next, to be detached at Exeter, then coaches for Exmouth and Sidmouth, to be detached respectively at Exmouth Junction and Sidmouth Junction, and finally a coach to be detached at Salisbury, to serve the intermediate stations between Salisbury and Seaton. There was no effort to maintain a strong Plymouth portion as the LSWR and its successor had abandoned Plymouth as a main destination ever since the shortening of the GWR route. The 'main' section of this train was the Ilfracombe portion, which, incidentally, also conveyed the GWR's Ilfracombe coach off the 'Cornish Riviera Limited', from Barnstaple Junction. The GWR did not have its own line to Ilfracombe, but had the right to pass its own vehicles over the Southern Railway's branch.

Water troughs were never laid on the LSWR, so a stop at Salisbury was necessary, even though Drummond had provided his locomotives with very large tenders. By the 1930s it was usual for the four-cylinder 'Lord Nelson' 4-6-0 locomotives to run between London and Salisbury, with two-cylinder 'King Arthurs', which were smaller but better suited for the Salisbury-Exeter line, to haul the train onwards. The stretch of line

ABOVE: Sir Lamiel, *the 'King Arthur' class locomotive which once hauled the 345-ton 'Atlantic Coast Express' at an average of 69mph between Salisbury and London. The picture shows it in excursion service after restoration.*

LEFT: Lord Nelson, *the first of a class which in the 1930s hauled the 'Atlantic Coast Express'. The wide 'Kylchap' chimney is a later addition.*

RIGHT: *'Clan Line', a rebuilt 'Merchant Navy', now restored for excursion use.*

between Salisbury and Exeter was unusual in being mainly straight or only gently curving, so there were virtually no speed restrictions, and the undulating profile of the track gave drivers every incentive to reach high speeds downhill so as to gain impetus for the uphill sections. Trains on this line frequently exceeded 80mph. Average speeds were therefore quite high, and despite the intermediate stops the 'Atlantic Coast Express' on the eve of World War II reached Exeter in just 3 hours 12 minutes, and Plymouth, 234 miles from London, in 5 hours 19 minutes. The marketing of the Southern Railway's seaside destinations was so successful that in the summer the train ran in two parts, and on summer Saturdays no fewer than eight parts were run, including two complete trains to the Ilfracombe line only, and several other parts to one or another branch line terminus.

The great days of the 'Atlantic Coast Express' ended with World War II, and its schedules were lengthened, despite the introduction of the new Bulleid 4-6-2 locomotives. From the 1940s, the 'Merchant Navy' Pacifics handled the train as far as Exeter. There, either 2-6-0 locomotives or the new 'West Country' 4-6-2s, scaled-down versions of the 'Merchant Navys', took over. From 1952, making use of the new locomotives, the train was accelerated and by 1961 the Waterloo-Salisbury section of nearly 84 miles was covered in 80 minutes. Between Salisbury and Exeter exceptionally high-speed schedules for such a hilly line were introduced, with, for example, 73 minutes for the 76 miles to Sidmouth Junction.

The 'Atlantic Coast Express' then began to die a slow death as first one, then another, of its constituent

LEFT, TOP: *The 'Bristolian', with its customary 'Castle' in charge, near Bath in 1956. The large numerals on the smokebox were introduced by the GWR to help signalmen identify approaching trains.*

LEFT: Tregenna Castle, *once a record-breaker with the 'Cheltenham Flyer', hauls a heavy South Wales train out of the Severn Tunnel.*

ABOVE: *Another 'Castle', one of a batch built after World War II, in charge of a London-Swansea train near Neath. The display on the left was the GWR's way of marking a permanent speed restriction.*

sections was eliminated. Finally, it ran only with Ilfracombe and Plymouth portions, and then disappeared altogether from the timetables. Soon after, also in the 1960s, the old LSWR line to Devon was downgraded to a secondary route. The LSWR's other main line, to Southampton, Bournemouth, and Weymouth, however, continued to flourish. Both the LSWR and its successor, the SR, operated Pullman services to Bournemouth, but the trains were not especially fast.

The 'Cornish Riviera Limited' and the 'Atlantic Coast Express' were primarily holiday trains, with somewhat reduced loadings in winter. Even more of a holiday train was the 'Torbay Express' of the GWR, for its principal destinations, Paignton and Kingswear (for the ferry to Dartmouth) were small settlements, owing their prosperity to tourism. Indeed, Paignton as a 'watering place' was very much a creation of GWR publicity. It was always a popular train, and before World War I, it was distinguished by the 4-vehicle section slipped at Taunton for Ilfracombe, which uniquely included a restaurant car. At that period the non-stop time to Exeter was three hours, reduced by eleven minutes by 1939. In its later decades this train was usually entrusted to a 'King' class locomotive, in view of its timing and heavy load, and this engine actually worked over the Kingswear branch. For England, this use of such a large passenger locomotive over a single-track branch was a very unusual spectacle.

Much less orientated towards holiday travel were the GWR's services to Bristol and to South Wales. The origins of the GWR were as a commercial link between the ports of London and Bristol, and its train service on this route was largely devoted to business travel. After

the construction of the Severn Tunnel, a new main line from Swindon to South Wales was developed, which passed via Badminton to the north of Bristol, but some London-Bristol trains also used it instead of the old route via Bath. The old route presented some quite difficult gradients to eastbound trains, and it was largely these which were routed back to London via the Badminton line, which at 118 miles was actually the same length.

The 'Bristolian', introduced in 1935, was one of those trains which ran via Bath in the westward direction and via Badminton for the return to London. It was a morning service from London, returning from Bristol in the late afternoon. Seven coaches was the original formation, hauled by a 'King', but such a 230-ton load, despite the tight schedule, was well within 'Castle' competence and that type of locomotive hauled the train for all but the first few months of its life. The coaches were wider than those of other railways, and again had the recessed end doors that the GWR had favoured in previous years. The schedule allowed 105 minutes, an average speed of 67mph, and the 'Bristolian' was the only regular GWR express without intermediate stops.

After the train's disappearance from the timetables in World War II it was restored to the 105-minute schedule in 1954, and in the last years of its life was diesel-hauled, and was eventually withdrawn as a named train in 1976. It did have a final fling with steam power, however, because in 1959 *Drysllwyn Castle* made the trip in 94 minutes, an exploit which encouraged the authorities to introduce a 100-minute timing when diesels took over. However, the diesels were unable to achieve this schedule reliably and it was soon put back to 105 minutes.

Express trains from London to South Wales were highly remunerative for the GWR, as there was plenty of traffic and long distances to be covered. Apart from the traffic bound for Ireland, this was a non-competitive route, but many improvements had been made to it in the first years of the century in order to provide a fast service to Fishguard, which was intended to become a port not only for Ireland but also for America, and which needed to have train services that could match those of the LNWR to Liverpool and Holyhead.

The first big improvement had been achieved two decades earlier, when the Severn Tunnel was finally completed. South Wales trains no longer needed to go all the way up to Gloucester and back down the northern shore of the River Severn. Then, from 1900, some avoiding lines were built. The Swansea avoiding line enabled trains to miss out the stop at Swansea, which was a terminal station necessitating a time-consuming train reversal. Then, even more ambitious, the Swansea District Lines took mainline Fishguard trains completely out of the Swansea and Neath areas, where lines were congested and steeply graded.

The normal express trains to South Wales were unnamed, ran fairly frequently, and were not especially fast, although they were typically quite heavy. Up to the Severn Tunnel, the line was fairly easily graded and well-engineered, but the long descent into the smoky Tunnel and the long climb out again were testing for locomotive men. Passenger trains were not usually given extra power for this section, although freight trains were doubleheaded through the Tunnel. At most periods, engines were changed at Cardiff, and for the 46 miles between Cardiff and Swansea an hour was usually allowed because of stiff gradients and speed restrictions due to

FAR LEFT: *The GWR tries to create a South Wales Riviera.*

LEFT: *In the difficult post-war years the railways had problems in accommodating peak holiday traffic, with results that were not quite those portrayed in this* Punch *cartoon.*

RIGHT: *The westbound 'Red Dragon' on arrival at Swansea. The 'Castle' locomotive is* Earl Cawdor, *named after a GWR director.*

BELOW: *Another view of the 'Red Dragon'. This picture shows the morning, London-bound, train.*

mining subsidence. Many trains terminated at Swansea, which was the last big industrial city on the route, but some were taken forward by an engine which backed down to their rear end in Swansea station. Llanelli was usually the next stop and at Carmarthen there was yet another reversal for trains proceeding westward to Fishguard or Pembroke Dock. Near the latter town, the GWR did much to develop Tenby as a holiday resort.

It was not until the days of British Railways that named trains began to circulate on the line to Cardiff and Swansea. The prime businessman's train, leaving Carmarthen at 7.30am and returning from London at 5.55pm, received the name of 'Red Dragon'. It was not an especially fast train, and anyone wishing to use it for a business trip had less than five hours in London. Another train of the same period, equally lethargic and heavy, was the 'Capitals United', linking London and Cardiff. But the 'Pembroke Coast Express', introduced in 1953, was far more sprightly and had the fastest-ever steam schedule to Newport, doing the 133 miles in 128 minutes and reaching Swansea in less than four hours. However, it did not move so fast west of Swansea, and probably did little to make Londoners feel that Tenby was well within reach as a holiday resort.

By the 1930s, after a period when the 'Saint' 2-cylinder 4-6-0s had done well on the South Wales trains, 4-cylinder 4-6-0s took over the main services. Before long the 'Castles' dominated the route. The larger 'Kings' were not allowed into South Wales until the very end of their lives, although the post-nationalisation 'Britannias' did replace some of the 'Castles' in the 1950s. West of Swansea, where loads were reduced, mixed-traffic locomotives of the 'Hall' and 'Grange' classes were often used, and coped well with the arduous climb for almost two miles up to Cockett Tunnel, where the inclination in parts was as steep as 1 in 52.

Another GWR service into Wales, almost exclusively aimed at holiday resorts, was the 'Cambrian Coast Express'. By the Railway Amalgamation of 1923 the GWR had absorbed the Cambrian Railway, an impecunious concern which had tried to make a sucess of its

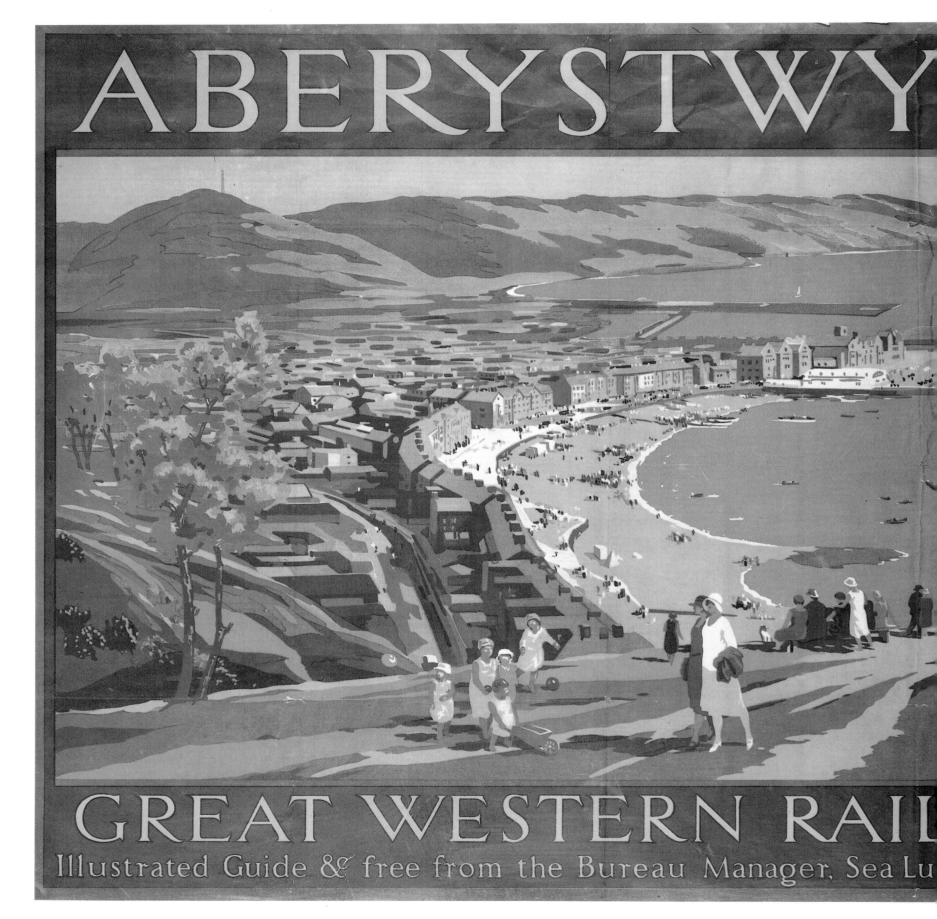

ABERYSTWY

GREAT WESTERN RAIL

Illustrated Guide & free from the Bureau Manager, Sea Lu

singletrack line through underpopulated Central Wales from Shrewsbury to Aberystwyth, Barmouth, and Pwllheli. Already, from 1921, the GWR had operated a summer-only train from London that went forward over the Cambrian to these coastal towns. The officially titled 'Cambrian Coast Express' appeared in 1927, and its exclusively holidaymaking character was manifested by its restriction to summer Fridays and Saturdays. The train was later cut back to Saturdays only, that being the day when seaside boarding houses changed their guests.

This train was quite fast up to Birmingham, then it coasted to Wolverhampton, where engines were changed. The Cambrian line engines were attached at

Wolverhampton, as Shrewsbury was avoided, and these were machines of low axle weight to suit the light track of that section. Old 'Duke' outside-framed 4-4-0s were often used, or one of the 'Dukedogs', which had been placed in service by the GWR in the 1930s to replace the 40-year-old 'Dukes', of which they were close copies.

Finally, when the train was restored after World War II, the new 'Manor' 4-6-0s were used on the Cambrian section. These were scaled-down versions of the standard GWR 2-cylinder 4-6-0, which were specially introduced for lines like the Cambrian. In these, its final days, the 'Cambrian Coast Express' was taking 6¼ hours for the London-Aberystwyth trip, short enough to

ABOVE: *Joint advertising by the railway company and seaside towns enabled the latter to advertise their attractions on scores of railway stations. Here is one of a long series of posters which helped to transform Aberystwyth into a major holiday resort.*

RIGHT, TOP: *A restored GWR 'Castle' and 'Hall' in excursion service on the Welsh Marches line.*

RIGHT: *One of the GWR 'Dukedog' 4-4-0 engines, now preserved. This type was introduced largely for services on the former Cambrian Railway's line to Aberystwyth.*

OVERLEAF: *Lydham Manor, one of the light 'Manor' 4-6-0 locomotives designed by the GWR for lines with weak bridges and track.*

43

GWR SPEED TO THE W
CORNWALL DEVON SOMERS

LEFT: *Perhaps the best-known of the GWR holiday posters, featuring a 'King' class locomotive.*

TOP: *A 'Castle' locomotive emerging from Cockett Tunnel, on the GWR's Swansea-Carmarthen line. The climb to Cockett was a little-publicised but very severe test for locomotivemen.*

ABOVE: *An Aberystwyth to Whitchurch train leaving Oswestry in the 1950s, hauled by a GWR 'Dukedog' 4-4-0.*

attract the most enthusiastic holidaymakers, but probably not short enough to persuade the doubtful. Aberystwyth, Barmouth and other Cambrian Coast resorts publicised by the GWR continued to get most of their holidaymakers from the industrial Midlands.

The GWR's most famous, even world-famous, train was the 'Cheltenham Flyer'. Cheltenham Spa was a town of great respectability and not one whose inhabitants would welcome the prospect of travelling to London at unheard-of speeds. The line itself did not lend itself to a short overall trip. From Cheltenham, trains proceeded to Gloucester, usually behind any mundane locomotive that happened to be available. At Gloucester the mainline locomotive was attached and then the train would continue to Swindon over a hilly and curving line through the Cotswolds. Only from Swindon, on the gently sloping line down to London, was a good speed possible, and in fact the high speed of the 'Cheltenham Spa Express' (as it was officially titled), was confined strictly to these last 77 miles.

It seems that it was more or less by chance that the GWR selected the afternoon train from Cheltenham as its runner in the high-speed stakes. Other trains might have been chosen, but the Cheltenham train was of fairly light weight, and it ran at a time when the main line was relatively clear of other trains. At that time, in 1923, the British start-to-stop record for a regularly scheduled train was held by the London & North Eastern Railway, successor to the North Eastern Railway, which had first won the record over the 44 miles from Darlington to York, which were then covered by one regular train in 43 minutes.

The GWR's first move was to reduce the 'Cheltenham Spa Express' timing from Swindon to London (Paddington) to 75 minutes, which entailed an average speed of 61.8mph. Then, in 1929, this was cut to 70 minutes, an average of 66mph. But in 1931 the Canadian Pacific Rail-

way robbed the GWR of its 'fastest regular run' title by accelerating one of its Montreal-Toronto trains to cover 124 miles in 108 minutes, an average of 68.9mph. The Great Western accepted this challenge by cutting three minutes off its schedule to raise the average speed to 69.2mph and then, in 1932, came a two-minute cut to raise the average to 71.4mph. This was the peak performance as far as regular scheduled running was concerned. For some time that 71.4mph speed remained a world record, but so great was the speed-up of train services in the mid-1930s that by 1939 the 'Cheltenham Spa Express' was not even in the top hundred on a world scale. This low ranking was largely due to the startling accelerations in the USA, but in Britain the LNER 'Coronation' had also beaten the Cheltenham train with its impressive 71.9mph schedule on the run between London and York.

On one occasion, when the 'Cheltenham Spa Express' was allowed to run as fast as was safe, irrespective of its official schedule, *Tregenna Castle* hauled the 200-ton six-coach train at an average of almost 82mph, and after the first five miles of acceleration and, before the last two miles of deceleration, kept up an average of 87.5mph. This, too, was a record until a few years later it was beaten by an LNER streamliner.

An unusual feature of the 'Cheltenham Spa Express' was that it ran in one direction only, the rolling stock returning to Cheltenham as an ordinary train. It was withdrawn in World War II and was never reinstated as a 'flyer'. Apart from its high speed, it was a good example of the Great Western express train, the coaches resplendent in their chocolate-and-cream livery, headed by a shining locomotive painted in Brunswick green, with its chimney's copper cap and its brass name- and number-plates brightly polished, and making little smoke thanks to the best Welsh steam coal that the GWR used for its locomotives.

ABOVE: Hinton Manor *in British Railways livery. This locomotive was one of the first modern locomotives to work on the Cambrian line to Aberystwyth, hauling the morning service from Oswestry. The picture shows it performing once again on that line after being restored for excursion service. Being suitable for mainline service, yet having a light axleload, the 'Manors' were ideal subjects for preservation, and almost a third of them were saved from the scrapper's torch.*

RIGHT: Llanstephan Castle, *one of the regular performers in the 'Cheltenham Flyer' service, brings that train into the GWR's Paddington terminus in 1937.*

MAIN LINES TO THE MIDLANDS

LEFT: *The 'South Yorkshireman', southbound on the former Great Central Railway's main line, pulls out of Rugby behind a B1 4-6-0.*

MAIN LINES TO THE MIDLANDS

For about 150 miles north of London, there is a belt of territory, never more than 50 miles wide, in which three mainline railways, the LNWR, Midland, and Great Northern, competed for traffic from the Midlands and South Yorkshire. There were few important towns in this belt which had less than two railways serving them, and a few, like Leeds, had three or more. Indeed, a railway enthusiast who was willing to lengthen his journey could have found a dozen different routes from London to places like Sheffield, Bradford and Nottingham.

At the end of the century an unexpected addition was made by the construction of yet another north-south trunk line in this overcrowded region. The new line was the Great Central. Formerly known as the Manchester, Sheffield and Lincolnshire Railway and carrying heavy freight traffic in its region, it decided to build a 'London Extension' and thereby join the big league of mainline railways. Its new line came south through Nottingham, Leicester and Rugby, tunnelled under the cricket pitch at Lords', and ended in a smart new terminus built at Marylebone.

This line was a triumph of nerve and imagination over reality, a reality reflected by the permanent absence of dividends on the GCR's ordinary shares after the London Extension was built. It was a railway which did not make a loss, perhaps, but made a very small profit that was immediately ploughed back into capital assets. In many ways the GCR trains and locomotives were the grandest in the country, and greatly appreciated by the public as such.

Nottingham and Sheffield were henceforth linked with London by the GNR, MR, and GCR. The LNWR lost its monopoly of Rugby-London traffic and Leicester people could choose between the GC and the Midland. The London-Sheffield traffic was a major object of competition, and it was one of several cases in Britain where a good traffic source was split between too many companies, so that none of them could make much profit from it. In the case of Sheffield, this was reflected by the several attempts to run non-stop London-Sheffield services. These had short lives because intermediate passengers were needed to provide the trains with a reasonable payload.

Before World War I the GCR's best train was the afternoon 'Sheffield Special', which ran non-stop over the 165 miles at an average of 56mph. Like many GCR expresses, it consisted of only five coaches, one of which was slipped at Leicester. Not so comfortable, but remarkably fast for those days, was the 2.45am newspaper train, whose vans were at first reserved for the *Daily Mail* and which provided some minimal passenger accommodation. It was typically a 150-ton train, and to maintain its schedules had to reach top speeds in the 75-85mph range.

In 1904, when the GCR was still accelerating its trains, the Midland responded by operating its London-Glasgow express non-stop to Sheffield, thereby reducing that 158-mile run to 3 hours 5 minutes. The Great Northern, to avoid being left behind, introduced a special evening express the following year which took only 2 hours 50 minutes. The GN route was 161 miles, about three miles shorter than the GC line, and the GCR replied by reducing its own schedule to 2 hours 50 minutes. But over the next few years both the GN and Midland introduced intermediate stops, only the GCR maintaining its non-stop schedule up to 1914, although, after the dis-

London to Birmingham: the fastest schedules

Year	GWR via Oxford (129 miles)	GWR via short route (110 miles)	LNWR/LMS (113 miles)
1888	3h 18m	—	2h 49m
1902	2h 20m	—	2h 0m
1910	—	2h 0m	2h 0m
1923	—	2h 0m	2h 0m
1939	—	2h 0m	1h 55m

Rival locomotives on the London-Birmingham-Wolverhampton route

Railway and class	Wheel arrangement	Cylinders (ins)	Coupled wheel diameter	Grate area (Sq ft)	Boiler pressure (psi)	Tractive effort (lbs)	Weight on coupled wheels (tons)
1914							
GWR Saint	4-6-0	18×30	6ft 8in	27	225	24,400	55
LNWR George V	4-4-0	20×26	6ft 9in	22	175	20,000	38
1939							
GWR Castle	4-6-0	(4) 16×26	6ft 8in	29	225	31,600	59
LMS Royal Scot	4-6-0	(3) 18×26	6ft 9in	31	250	33,150	63

appearance of effective competition, the timing was lengthened to 2 hours 57 minutes. Interestingly, the 'Sheffield Special' (which never bore that name officially) was actually bound for destinations beyond Sheffield. The main part continued to Manchester, slipping a coach for Bradford on the way, and the hardest part of the trip was just beyond Sheffield, where the line leading to the Woodhead Tunnel consisted of 18 miles of grades that could be as steep as 1 in 120.

The Great Central locomotives were as handsome as the coaches and were distinguished by their well-proportioned look and large boilers. In its early days the 'Sheffield Special' was hauled by a 4-4-0, and then by the 4-4-2 engines designed by the GC locomotive superintendent JG Robinson. Later, Robinson's 'Directors' were used. These were one of the most remarkable 4-4-0 designs in Britain. Simple in construction, with large but fairly short boilers, they were capable of work which on other railways would have been entrusted to a 4-6-0. The GCR did possess some 4-6-0s for its heavier trains, and these were notable in that they were built in a series of very small classes, of from two to fourteen units each, and differed from each other mainly in the size of their driving wheels. As the 'Directors' were so good for passenger trains, most of the 4-6-0s were designed with smallish wheels suitable for fast freight. The largest class of these, of 14 units with 6ft driving wheels, was ideal for rushing fish trains down from Grimsby to London.

In World War I, the 'Sheffield Special' was one of the few trains which continued to offer a restaurant car. It included stops at Leicester, Nottingham and Penistone which, on a schedule only slightly lengthened, entailed some hard work for the locomotive. After the Railway

RIGHT, TOP: Earl Beatty *belonged to the last, but probably not the best, design of Great Central passenger 4-6-0 locomotives. This class received names connected with the Great War.*

RIGHT, CENTRE: Butler Henderson, *a Great Central 4-4-0 of the very successful 'Director' class. This locomotive is now preserved. Built in 1920, it was the forerunner of a class of 35 units, some of which were built by the GCR's successor, the LNER, for Scottish lines.*

RIGHT, BOTTOM: Mayflower, *a preserved example of the LNER B1 class of mixed-traffic 4-6-0. It is shown painted in LNER green livery, but it was originally black, like the rest of the class.*

Amalgamation, the GCR became part of the new LNER, and the latter re-equipped the train with new standard rolling stock, enlarging it to a 7-car formation of about 250 tons. In due course, the LNER 'Sandringham' class 4-6-0s replaced the 'Directors' and in 1939 the train finally disappeared from the timetables.

After World War II, however, two officially named trains appeared on the former GC London Extension. One of these was the 'Master Cutler', a morning service from Sheffield to London with an evening return. Compared to the pre-war schedules, it was a slow train, but it was convenient and, moreover, faster than the competing train over the Midland Railway's successor, the LMS. The second train, the 'South Yorkshireman', was the successor of the GCR's and LNER's evening train from London to Bradford, with the return working at 10am from Bradford. Like the 'Master Cutler', its schedule was somewhat longer than the corresponding pre-war train, although, with its usual ten coaches, it was considerably heavier. Both trains were hauled not by express engines, but by the new B1 class of mixed-traffic 4-6-0 and this, together with the use of standard rolling stock, suggested that these trains belonged to the post-war series of named trains whose titles were little more than a public relations gesture, named in the hope that if a train was said to be good, then it would become good. Interestingly, this did happen in most cases, since railwaymen would pay especial attention to the turn-out and timekeeping of these trains.

Before 1914, the Midland Railway, although it could not beat the Great Central timings to Sheffield, made a good showing to Nottingham, where it served London with fifteen daily non-stop runs. Having a shorter route of 124 miles than the Great Central's 126, and more easily graded as well, it could offer a 2-hour 12-minute schedule while the GCR could do no better than 2 hours 23 minutes. Despite the favourable conditions, however, it was not on this route that the MR ran its fastest train before 1914; this was achieved over the 31 miles between Appleby and Carlisle on the Settle and Carlisle line, which one train covered at an average of 56mph. When, finally, a named train, the 'Robin Hood', was introduced between London (St Pancras) and Nottingham in 1959, it took 2 hours 10 minutes, which was little better than the MR's schedule.

A named train introduced by the LMS over the Midland route was the 'Yorkshireman', from London to Bradford, which did the London to Sheffield section in 3 hours 10 minutes. This train was remarkable among those serving the East Midlands and South Yorkshire for its introduction of novel rolling stock. It was the first of the LMS Railway's trains formed entirely of central-aisle, open-plan coaches. The LMS in the inter-war period built many such coaches, but whether the public preferred them to the traditional compartment layout was doubtful.

The GCR came no closer to Birmingham than Rugby, but with its co-operation, the GWR was able to compete on equal terms with the LNWR for the lucrative Birmingham traffic.

The LNWR route from London to Birmingham, apart from the initial climb out from the Euston terminus, was easily graded and, at 113 miles, fairly direct. The GWR route was also easily graded, as it followed the Thames Valley for much of its length. But the Thames, unfortunately, did not flow at all near Birmingham, so the GWR line was somewhat circuitous at almost 130 miles. Moreover, south of Birmingham, it climbed for over

three miles up to Hatton, at gradients of around 1 in 110.

To all intents and purposes, therefore, the LNWR dominated the through London-Birmingham passenger service by virtue of the shorter travelling times it offered. In 1902, it enhanced this attraction by introducing the first two-hour schedule, and within a couple of years it offered three non-stop trains in each direction which took just two hours.

Coventry was served by slip coaches which, unusually, were not allowed to enter the platform by their own momentum but were pulled in by a shunting unit, often a horse. In 1913 these slip coaches were further distinguished by being provided with vestibule connections. On other railways, from fear that slip-coach passengers might find themselves in the wrong coach at slipping time, these connections had not been fitted. The Coventry passengers were thus able to use the restaurant car, if they took good care to be back in their slip coach well before Coventry.

The GWR did make a great effort, but it never succeeded in scheduling a train to Birmingham via its Oxford route at less than 2 hours 17 minutes. Soon after the Great Central reached London in 1899, it found that the

ABOVE: Ramillies, *a compound 4-4-0, pulls away with an LNWR express train. The photograph was probably taken around 1905, the engine having been built in 1900 but given a new, square, Belpaire firebox in 1904. More effective 'Precursor' 4-4-0 locomotives would have taken over the haulage of this train within a few years after the picture was taken.*

RIGHT, TOP: *An LNER B1 4-6-0 at Perth. Being built during and after the War, this class of engine was usually in a black and grimy condition, as here.*

RIGHT: *A pair of 'Jubilee' 4-6-0 locomotives at rest in the old Euston Station in 1947, after bringing in a train from Liverpool. Many of this numerous class of locomotives were named after parts of the British Empire; the leading engine here is* Palestine.

part of its line which it shared with the Metropolitan Railway was becoming too congested to handle fast trains. The GWR and GCR then co-operated in building a jointly owned line which would provide a shorter route to the north for the GWR, and a less-congested route to its own, different, north, for the GCR.

The jointly owned part was about 32 miles long, and the GWR built sundry sections to fill in gaps to create a new main line from Old Oak Common, in west London, to a junction with its old London-Birmingham line near Banbury. The whole scheme was completed in 1910. In anticipation of these changes the LNWR had improved its services, and, in 1910, it introduced its 'City-to-City' service designed for businessmen. This train, instead of starting from Euston, had its terminus in the heart of the commercial district, at Broad St Station. But it was this feature, intended to boost traffic, which seems to have been the main deterrent. City types did not like to change their ways and preferred to take a cab to Euston than to catch the train on their own doorstep. Other inducements offered by this train included a typewriting compartment, complete with typist, and a restaurant car. This car represented a quarter of the train, which was of four vehicles only and, failing to attract the necessary custom, was discontinued after a few years.

The new GWR route was only 110 miles, and immediately on opening carried two-hour London to Bir-

mingham services. Although shorter than the LNWR route, the new line was more heavily graded, and hard work was required of the locomotives. Slip coaches were employed to avoid intermediate stops at both Banbury and Leamington, and another was dropped at Knowle, in the Birmingham businessman's residential district.

In World War I, the GWR and LNWR schedules were lengthened, and trains began to make proper stops at Coventry. In the post-war years, the two-hour timing was restored, but the LMS trains, formerly LNWR, henceforth made several intermediate stops. Coventry, for example, was developing as a motor industry centre and needed an improved train service. More powerful locomotives enabled these stops to be absorbed without lengthening the timings. In the 1920s the LMS was dominated by a Midland faction in its locomotive department, and it was not long before the LNWR 'George the Fifths' were taken off the Birmingham trains and replaced by Midland 'Compounds'. These were in their turn ousted by the much bigger 3-cylinder 'Jubilee' class 4-6-0s in the 1930s. But later other 4-6-0s, of the 'Patriot' and 'Royal Scot' classes, took over most of the trains. The larger LMS engines of the 4-6-2 wheel arrangement were not used for these trains, not because high power outputs were unwanted, but because there were engineering restrictions on their movement over the Birmingham line.

After World War II, the 2-hour schedules were slow

ABOVE: *The new LMS Royal Scot locomotive on exhibition at Euston Station soon after construction in 1927. Although this class of locomotive was an enormous improvement on its predecessors, the design was not outstanding.*

RIGHT, TOP: *One of the 'Royal Scot' locomotives,* The King's Royal Rifle Corps, *enters Birmingham's New Street Station with a London express. This class was rebuilt with a new taper boiler and double chimney, producing some fine performances.*

RIGHT: *A Midland Railway 4-4-0 of a 1912 design, photographed at Birmingham in 1948.*

to reappear, but with the use of 'Royal Scot' haulage they were reinstated and in 1953 the 'Midlander' was introduced, which covered the 94 miles between Coventry and London in 94 minutes.

In the 1950s, the 'Cambrian Coast Express' had a daily 2-hour schedule between London and Birmingham on the GWR route. It had been joined by another named train, the 'Inter-City', a title which was later adopted by British Rail as a general marketing slogan. In 1951, Festival of Britain year, another London-Birmingham-Wolverhampton train, named the 'William Shakespeare', carried through coaches for Stratford-on-Avon, which were dropped at Leamington for movement over the Stratford branch.

The demands made on locomotives over the Great Western route were much greater than those faced by the competing LNWR and LMS locomotives. Apart from Hatton Bank, there were long climbs through the Chilterns which, however, were typically breasted at about 50mph, despite the heavy loads. In the 1950s, characteristic loadings were 13 coaches, and with a weight of around 400 tons, top speeds of up to 90mph were common while descending the gradients.

It is doubtful whether the GWR could have introduced 2-hour timings had it not been for the locomotive revolution which occurred on that railway in the first decade of the century. It was George Churchward, the locomotive superintendent of the GWR from 1902 to 1921, who by taking the best of British, American and French practice, plus a few ideas of his own or of his assistants, was mostly responsible for transforming design concepts, which would subsequently affect other British railways. He constructed a range of distinctive locomotives that were able to substantially out-perform their contemporaries.

Churchward's 4-6-0 No 98 set the pattern. Built in 1902, it used an American-style outside-cylinder layout, which eliminated the cranked axle of inside-cylinder types, which was notoriously difficult to manufacture. Churchward refined the Continental Belpaire square firebox by giving it stronger corners and wider spaces for the water to circulate. His cylinders had an exceptionally long piston travel of 30 inches, a factor often wrongly criticised by those who overlooked the corresponding long travel of the steam admission valves. This long valve travel permitted large steam admission ports to the

cylinders, so that steam from the boiler no longer needed to be 'throttled' at its passage into and out of the cylinder. The clear-cut exhaust, with no hint of muffle, which shot out of GWR chimneys when locomotives were working hard, demonstrated the smartness with which the steam was handled.

The long smokebox, with the chimney set well back, was another American feature, and the all-important proportions of chimney and blastpipe were calculated on the basis of academic research done in America. Externally, apart from the very exposed wheels and the profusion of polished brass which enhanced the green paintwork, the most prominent feature was the long tapered boiler; this distinguished future GWR locomotives from those of other companies. It had no dome but only a distinctive haycock-shaped safety-valve cover. Tapering the boiler saved weight and also ensured that the all-important firebox end was kept well supplied with water.

Easton Court, *a two-year old 'Saint' class engine of the GWR, hauls a varied collection of rolling stock forming the evening Shrewsbury-Bristol train in 1914.*

INSET: *The final development of the 'Saint' two-cylinder 4-6-0 was the 'County' class of 1945. Here* County of Cardigan *storms Hatton Bank with a train destined for Birmingham.*

The boiler pressure of Churchward locomotives, typically 225psi, was somewhat higher than the usual 180psi. Although it placed a greater strain on the boiler, the higher pressure had everything to recommend it as it produced greater power and also enabled the boiler to hold a bigger reserve for those difficult stretches where steam consumption outpaced steam production. No 98 soon showed that it was in advance of needs, but it was not long before train speed and weight were sufficiently advanced to exploit this new breed of locomotive. No 98 was developed into the very successful 'Saint' class of 2-cylinder 4-6-0, and it was these engines which made a success of the pre-1914 2-hour Birmingham expresses as

well as distinguishing themselves on the other GWR main lines. It was 'Saint Bartholomew', working one of the Birmingham trains and hauling 320 tons, which maintained 90mph over at least 1¼ miles while descending from Beaconsfield towards London.

Churchward, always an experimenter, tried the compound principle not by designing his own compound locomotives but by importing three well-reputed examples from France. After lengthy trials, he decided that they were not superior to his own single-expansion locomotives after the latter had been fitted with steam superheaters. This finding did much to kill enthusiasm for compounds in Britain. Churchward also built some of

ABOVE: *One of the first 'Star' class engines,* Rising Star, *hauls a GWR mainline express in 1935, 28 years after its entry into service. Locomotives of this type were regularly used in the London-Worcester service up to the 1950s.*

his 4-6-0 locomotives as, initially, 4-4-2s, to compare the two wheel arrangements. He finally decided that the extra adhesion offered by six as opposed to four driving wheels was, for the GWR at least, more important than the better firebox design possible with the 4-4-2. For the rest of its life the GWR, with one solitary 4-6-2 exception, built only 4-6-0 locomotives for its mainline passenger trains.

For extra power, demanded in particular by the west of England expresses, Churchward introduced a 4-cylinder version of his 'Saints'. This became known as the 'Star' class, the first unit being 'North Star', and was a remarkably successful locomotive design which remained in mainline service into the 1950s.

Aesthetically, Churchward's breed of locomotive had an interesting public response. To all generations it announced that GWR locomotives were something different, but at the time of their first appearance they were regarded as stark, ugly and un-British. Certainly they were more angular than their rotund predecessors, and their blatant exposure of wheels and cylinders was alien

to a society that had just invented Victorian propriety. But within a few decades, and especially in the last years of steam, the GWR locomotive was regarded as something representing the best of British engineering and the best of British taste. The sight of a green GWR 4-6-0 going steamily but almost smokelessly up Hatton Bank with a chocolate-and-cream train behind it was a spectacle which, once seen, was long remembered.

Churchward was succeeded by Charles Collett, whose management of GWR locomotive affairs between the wars was virtually a matter of building on what Churchward had founded. From the 'Stars' he developed the 'Castles', which were simply scaled-up versions of the former and which became a classic locomotive design thanks to their exploits on the 'Cheltenham Flyer' and to their multiplication to a point where they handled almost all the main GWR expresses. In turn, Collett enlarged the 'Castles' to produce the 'Kings'. These were intended for the especially heavy duties, like the trains to Plymouth, which faced the severe South Devon gradients, and the heavier Birmingham trains.

RIGHT: *A 'Star' class engine leaving Swansea with a stopping train to Bristol. This photograph was taken in the 1950s, the last decade of this type's life.*

Both on the LMS and the GWR, the London to Birmingham trains did not terminate at that Midland city.
The LNWR (later LMS) trains continued as far as Wolverhampton, while the GWR trains also went there, but
usually continued up to Shrewsbury, Chester, and Birkenhead. At Wolverhampton, the GWR trains changed
engines, 'Kings' not being allowed further north and
'Castles' being regarded as too good a class to be used on
what was really a secondary service. For a long period,
therefore, while the three 'Kings' stationed at Wolverhampton, helped by sister-engines based in London,
handled the heaviest trains as far as Wolverhampton, the
responsibility for the northern continuation was borne by
the elderly 'Saints' which in pre-1914 days had handled
the duties that the 'Kings' and 'Castles' were currently
performing. The longevity of British locomotive types,
on the GWR and elsewhere, owed much to the way
further use could be found for locomotives that time and
progress had rendered unsuitable for their original
duties.

RIGHT: *A GWR London to
Birkenhead express climbing
Hatton Bank, hauled by
King George II .*

ABOVE: *The biggest and smallest of the GWR family of 4-6-0:* King George V, *with the double chimney fitted to all 'Kings' in their later years, leads 'Manor' class locomotive* Hinton Manor, *on a 1985 excursion celebrating the 150th anniversary of the Great Western Railway.*

LEFT: *The GWR was very proud of its 30 'Kings', and lost no opportunity of publicising them with photographs like this.*

BOAT
TRAINS

LEFT: *Cross-Channel passengers make a simple train-to-ship transfer at Dover Docks, having been hauled from London by a Wainwright 4-4-0 of the SECR. The steamer is SS* Engadine.

As Britain is an island, it was natural that many railway companies offered boat train services to the passenger ports around the country. These ports were of three types: those which despatched boats to British offshore islands like the Isles of Wight and Man; those which sent somewhat larger ships to continental ports; and those which handled ocean liners. The first category also included the several services to Ireland, while the Continental services, although primarily short-sea routes to ports like Calais or Ostend, also included longer journeys to Scandinavia and Germany.

One of the most famous trains was the LNWR's 'Irish Mail', which ran from London along the North Wales coast to Holyhead. This was probably the first train in the world to have an official name, a name which, incidentally, was purely factual. The first run was in summer 1848, and departure time was 8.45pm, which allowed the London sorting offices to deliver their mailbags to Euston Station in time to ensure that a letter posted in London in the late afternoon could be delivered in Dublin the next day.

Although passengers were carried, the prime function of this train was to carry mail. In many countries, including Britain, the fast carriage of mail was considered by governments to be a prime function of the railways, which were expected to carry the mails at very low rates and on very demanding schedules. On the other hand, the government mail contracts were a sure source of income in bad times as well as good, and there were many cases where a train service survived only because it could rely on such income. In Britain, as in some other countries, the mail trains included sorting vans where post office workers could expedite delivery by sorting letters *en route*. Britain also developed lineside pick-up and setting-down apparatus whereby mail pouches could be dropped or collected without the train stopping or even slowing down.

It was for the 'Irish Mail' that this mail-exchange gear was first devised. Dublin was, at the time, a vital British city and was required to have the best possible communications with the mainland. The mail contracts specified extremely demanding schedules, which not only impelled the LNWR to pick up mail at speed but also to develop water troughs so that the train could run long distances without stopping for water as well. The world's first troughs at Conway, on the main line to Holyhead, were installed after a Post Office statement that in 1860 an average speed of 42mph would be demanded between London and the quay at Holyhead. It was bad luck that the winter of 1860-61 was one of the hardest that could be remembered. Not only did the water troughs freeze up, but metal parts of the rolling stock fractured because of the extremely low temperatures. The Post Office was relatively understanding over these difficulties, but even in the best of times the stiff requirements meant that the LNWR suffered very high costs in operating this train.

By 1880, the Irish connection was considered so vital that a new dock was opened at Holyhead by the Prince of Wales. Trains could henceforth stop beside the steamers, which was an improvement for the passengers although they still had to transfer between the train and ship in the small hours as the train ran to suit the Post Office, and nobody else. Passengers valuing their sleep were happier on the morning train for Holyhead which, in LMS days at least, was renowned for its excellent restaurant car service.

It was after the LMS had absorbed the LNWR that

Boat trains by the Southern Railway's 'Short Sea Route' in 1939		
Departure London Victoria	Arrival at quay	Connection
09.00	10.42 Folkestone	Paris
10.30	12.55 Dover	Brussels
11.00	12.35 Dover	Paris (Golden Arrow)
14.00	15.35 Dover	Paris
15.00	16.55 Dover	Brussels
16.30	18.09 Folkestone	Paris
22.00	23.37 Dover	Paris (Night Ferry)
23.00	01.00 Dover	Brussels

LEFT, TOP: *A postal car used for the 'Ocean Mail' service of the GWR.*

LEFT: *A mail pouch suspended outside a travelling post office vehicle, and about to be seized by a railside pick-up arm.*

ABOVE: *The 'Irish Mail' in about 1910. The 'Precursor' class locomotive is about to pick up water from the track troughs.*

RIGHT: *The 'Irish Mail' in the final days of steam, hauled by a British Railways 'Britannia' Pacific.*

the name 'Irish Mail' at last began to be carried on the train itself, which was also equipped with some fine new sleeping cars. But sleeping car passengers still had to rouse themselves for Holyhead quay at 2am.

With the Irish troubles of the 1920s, traffic fell off, but the train continued to run. By 1939, it was again very heavy, often comprising 16 vehicles with the 500-ton load entrusted to one of the 'Royal Scot' locomotives. In its final steam-hauled days, the 'Irish Mail' was still scheduled to leave Euston at 8.45pm, but arrived at Holyhead only at 2.25am. Before the War, a fast relief section of the train had been run at busy periods and managed the 264 miles in 5 hours 10 minutes.

The route of the 'Irish Mail' was by no means the only way to reach Ireland. The LNWR itself had a share in the railway giving access to Stranraer harbour in southwestern Scotland, the other owners being the Midland Railway and the two Scottish companies, the Caledonian and the Glasgow & South Western. The Midland and LNWR, and the Caledonian and GSWR, were normally distrustful of each other, but in the case of Stranraer they had a common interest in making a success of the port. From Stranraer steamers plied to Larne in northern Ireland, and they had, for many passengers, the priceless virtue of spending only an hour in the open sea, half the trip being in the sheltered waters of Loch Ryan. The MR ran the best service to Stranraer from London by attaching a sleeping car and some coaches to its late evening London-Leeds train. After the Railway Amalgamation, the new LMS re-routed the service, attaching the Stranraer coaches to one of the West Coast Anglo-Scottish trains. During World War II, partly because this short sea route was less exposed to submarine attack, it became very important, and two sleeping car expresses ran nightly to Stranraer from London.

The last section of the line to Stranraer through Dumfries was known as the 'Port Road', and was a difficult line to work because of its severe gradients. In the 1950s, the night train was given the name 'Northern Irishman' and was one of a very small number of trains to be hauled by one of the 'Clan' class light Pacifics built by British Railways.

The Stranraer line was also the natural route for travellers to Ireland from Scotland and northern England. The Glasgow & South Western, never one of Britain's greatest railways, made a big effort with its 'Irishman' and the summer-only 'Fast Belfast' from Glasgow to Stranraer. With the 'Irishman', the passenger could leave Belfast at 6.25pm and, weather permitting, be in Glasgow by midnight. In the other direction he was not so lucky, because for operating reasons the 'Irishman' set him down at Stranraer before 11pm whereas the boat did not leave until 6.30am. Both trains were limited to six vehicles because of the severe gradients, including almost four miles of 1 in 55 up to Pinmore Tunnel. The GSWR used its handsome 4-4-0 locomotives on these trains, but, after the Railway Amalgamation, these were succeeded first by Midland compound 4-4-0s, then by LMS 2-6-0s, and later by 4-6-0s.

The Midland Railway, not content with its service via Stranraer, hankered after its own, fully-owned, port for the Irish service. Its plans came to fruition with the almost simultaneous acquisition of the Belfast & Northern Counties Railway in Ireland (which it renamed the Northern Counties Committee) in 1903, and the opening of its new harbour at Heysham, near Morecambe, in 1904. The MR's Belfast boat train left London at 6pm and covered the 268 miles to Heysham in just less than six hours. It ran in almost direct competition with a service jointly operated by the LNWR and Lancashire & Yorkshire railways, which ran from London to connect with a Belfast boat at Fleetwood.

Eventually, under LMS auspices, the Fleetwood service was dropped in favour of the more modern facilities at Heysham, but the Heysham boat trains were removed from former MR tracks and taken north over the former LNWR. By this time, in the late 1920s, the Belfast train was called the 'Ulster Express'. It became a very ordinary, unnamed, train during World War II, but was reinstated and remained in service until the Heysham-Belfast steamer was withdrawn in 1975.

Another named train on this route, virtually unknown to all except its patrons, was the 'Belfast Boat Express' which ran to Heysham from Manchester; this had the distinction of of being British Railways' last steam-hauled named train.

ABOVE: *The GWR's Fishguard Harbour station in 1908. In the foreground a train of steam coal awaits transfer to the dockside bunkers.*

LEFT: *A big day for Fishguard Harbour in August 1909 with the docking of the transatlantic SS Mauretania. The picture shows the first boat special leaving for London behind a pair of outside-framed 4-4-0s. A travelling locomotive inspector can be seen on the footplate of the leading engine,* Halifax.

RIGHT: *The record-breaking GWR Duke of Connaught, which distinguished itself hauling the 'Ocean Mail' in 1904.*

Yet another grasp for the Anglo-Irish traffic was made by the Great Western Railway, which, in 1906, blasted away hundreds of tons of rock to build a station at Fishguard in southwest Wales. From here, day and night steamers were operated to another new port at Rosslare in southeastern Ireland. This gave the GWR an advantage for the southern Irish traffic and connecting restaurant car trains were run from Rosslare to Waterford and Cork. Moreover, the new development provided a viable alternative route to Dublin over the Dublin and South Eastern Railway. Boat trains left London in the morning and evening, and were timed to cover the 261 miles in 5½ hours. The trains, which were initially hauled by outside-frame 4-4-0s until the new 4-6-0s took over, carried restaurant cars, and the night train provided sleepers for first-class passengers. Despite such comfort, the first-class passengers, just like their fellow-travellers on the 'Irish Mail', had to relinquish their cosy berths soon after 2am when the train drew alongside the boat.

Fishguard was expected to become a great transatlantic port when the Cunard Company began to schedule a call there for its New York ships on their way to and from Liverpool. Passengers disembarking at Fishguard could reduce the New York-London transit by about a day. The GWR was so excited at this prospect that, apart from providing very good boat trains, it also built new lines around Swansea to provide a clearer run. But the GWR's old rival, the London & South Western, won the last trick by building its huge dock complex at Southampton. When Cunard, realising that a Southampton terminal gave a chance for its liners to pick up French traffic at Cherbourg, transferred much of its fleet to the new port, Fishguard lost its future as a transatlantic port.

Liverpool and the LNWR also suffered from the competition of Southampton, although Cunard, Canadian Pacific, and other big companies continued to send some ships to Liverpool. The first blow for the LNWR had been the transfer of the Inman Line ships to Southampton in 1893. These were big ships, and their names were carried by a pair of LNWR locomotives – the Railway named some of its engines after ships using its ports.

The LNWR responded by improving its facilities and built a tunnel and a line that enabled its boat trains to draw up alongside the liners at the new Riverside Station. This improvement was inaugurated in 1895 when a special train was run to connect with the departure of the White Star *Germanic* to New York. The Liverpool press pointed out, not entirely fairly, that New York was fourteen hours closer to London via Liverpool than via Southampton.

By 1914 the LNWR, because of the increased scale of transatlantic travel, was handling unprecedented numbers of boat trains to and from Liverpool. For a ship like the *Mauretania*, three special trains would be run from London, departing one after the other inside an hour and averaging 55mph over the main line. At Edge Hill, in Liverpool, the mainline run ended as a couple of small tank engines took the train slowly down to the Riverside Station. Usually, a liner would leave about one hour after the last train had arrived.

In its efforts to stave off the threat of Southampton, in 1908 the LNWR introduced new trains which, if not the most magnificent, were certainly the most distinctive to be seen on British railways at that time. Once the decision was made that the so-called 'American Specials' should have specially-designed rolling stock, something

out of the ordinary was guaranteed. These were eight-car trains, where each car matched the others in profile, and combined the best of British coachbuilding with American features, thereby making the transatlantic visitor feel at home. The coaches were 65ft 6in long, with elliptical roofs rather than the clerestory types used elsewhere in the LNWR. The internal layout was un-American, having compartments and side corridors, but some first-class compartments had American-style armchairs instead of the usual seats. All the passenger-carrying vehicles ran on 6-wheel bogies, with the kitchen car and the two luggage vans having conventional 4-wheel bogies. The heavy bogies, the tight couplings, and above all the superb LNWR mainline track provided a ride far smoother than Americans were used to.

After the LNWR had become part of the LMS, the Liverpool boat trains continued to run, although it was not long before the special rolling stock was replaced by good, but standard, LMS vehicles on 4-wheel bogies. The practice of showing interest in this traffic by naming locomotives after transatlantic liners declined under LMS management, but was revived after nationalisation, with some new diesel locomotives taking well-known Cunarder names.

At one time, Plymouth seemed well-placed to handle transatlantic liners, and in fact the occasional

RIGHT: *The official photograph of the record-breaking City of Truro, which reached 100mph when hauling a GWR 'Ocean Mail' train in 1904.*

BELOW: City of Truro *in the third phase of its life, hauling an excursion in Yorkshire in 1986. Previously, this engine had been exhibited at the original railway museum in York, and then at the Swindon railway museum before being restored for active service. In the late 1950s, between excursions, it was also used for ordinary services.*

French Line (CGT) ship called up to the end of the 1960s. Both the LSWR and the GWR did what they could to foster this traffic by providing boat trains to London. At first, their competition was muted, as there was a kind of gentleman's agreement whereby the LSWR would provide a special train for passengers between Plymouth and London, while the GWR would occupy itself with the mail. In this latter connection the GWR was, for once, a beneficiary of its circuitous route, for, by calling at Bristol, its ocean mail trains could drop mail for Birmingham and the north. For the LSWR, the ocean passenger traffic was probably unprofitable, although with the accounting procedures of that time, the Company was, most likely, unaware of this. Not only did it have to keep high-class rolling stock available for these occasional one-way trips, but that same rolling stock had to include sleeping cars because liners might arrive at any hour of day or night.

The agreed traffic division was no deterrent against engaging in yet another railway 'race', the last as it happened. On the face of it, it was absurd that the two companies should struggle to arrive first in London when only one of them was carrying passengers. The explanation, probably, is that the GWR after decades of lethargy was, by 1904, seeking to regain its position as Britain's most prestigious railway.

Its exploits with the 'Ocean Mail' were not the first manifestations of its resolve to break speed records. Although in 1902 the new Churchward engines had hardly made their debut, some remarkably good 4-4-0s had been built, and in March 1902 a royal train to Devon gave the GWR its first opportunity to show what it could do. Under Queen Victoria, the royal trains, luxuriously furnished, were expected to proceed at a sedate pace, but with the accession of her ebullient son Edward VII things changed. The March 1902 royal train ran non-stop from London to Kingswear and with five vehicles the 4-4-0 *Britannia* averaged 56mph to Exeter and 52mph to Kingswear, the train running non-stop the whole way. This was an impressive performance and what was particularly important was that the King showed great enthusiasm for it, encouraging the GWR to go one better when the Prince of Wales visited Cornwall in 1903. A train of three saloons was provided, headed by a 'City' class 4-4-0, *City of Bath*. This class had the advantage of carrying Churchward's tapered boiler which provided high steam output over long runs. Down Dauntsey Bank, this train reached 87mph, and Bristol was passed in 1¾ hours from Paddington. Then, over the Somerset levels the train averaged 75mph between Bristol and Taunton, so that Exeter was passed in 172 minutes from London, an average of 67mph. Despite the south Devon gradients, Plymouth was reached at an average of 63mph, which remained a record for several decades.

With this well-publicised success, it is hardly surprising that the GWR resolved to make other record-breaking runs, and the 'Ocean Mail' was chosen, for the added glory of beating the LSWR's Plymouth boat train. The GWR route from Plymouth as far as Exeter was five miles shorter than the LSWR's, although this was more than compensated by the 20 extra miles the GW train had to run between Exeter and London.

The LSWR did not handle this competition very

RIGHT: *Boat trains from Folkestone Harbour faced a severe gradient on the branch up to Folkestone Junction, where the mainline engine was attached. Here a trio of former SECR tank locomotives begin the stiff haul from the docks.*

BELOW: *Combined timetable and publicity material of the Wagons-Lits organisation in 1900.*

BELOW, RIGHT: *Passengers leave the post-war 'Golden Arrow' at Dover Marine to join the ferry.*

FEBRUARY, 1900.

THE CONTINENTAL TRAVELLER

The official Journal, Time Book & Guide of the INTERNATIONAL SLEEPING CAR & EUROPEAN EXPRESS TRAINS Co, and of the INTERNATIONAL PALACE COMPANY, (Cᵉ Iⁿᵗˡᵉ DES GRANDS HÔTELS)

Published Monthly, at the London Offices of the Company, 14, Cockspur Street, S.W.

well. It decided to change engines at Templecombe instead of Salisbury, and between Plymouth and Templecombe used new big-boilered 4-4-0s which were ideal for the gradients west of Exeter but not for the high speeds needed to the east of that station. The fastest LSWR run recorded was in 1904, when a Drummond T9 4-4-0, hauling four coaches, or about 100 tons, ran the 112 miles from Templecombe to London Waterloo in 104 minutes, an average of 64mph. This was not a particularly high speed in the circumstances and the only exciting part of the trip was the perilous hurtle around the curve at Salisbury at a speed well in excess of what was allowed.

A month later the GWR produced an outstanding run, which was to be the peak performance of Edwardian Britain. Including almost four minutes at Bristol to change engines and detach the mail van for the north, the 'Ocean Mail' ran from Plymouth to London in just 3 hours 47 minutes. For the first leg, *City of Truro* was in charge, and dashed over the winding grades of South Devon between Plymouth and Exeter at an average of 57mph. This in itself was exciting, but then on the descent of Wellington Bank, near Taunton, *City of Truro* was timed at 102mph over a quarter mile. Such timing, taken with a stop-watch against mileposts, was not precise, but after some controversy it was accepted that a speed of 100mph was most probably reached at this point. This was a record so startling that the GWR decided that it would not be in its best interests to give it wide publicity. The continuation east of Bristol was behind a Single, *Duke of Connaught*, which covered the 118 miles in less than 100 minutes with the four remaining mail vans. For 70 miles of this sector, the average speed was 80mph, a record which remained until the coming of the 'Cheltenham Flyer' decades later.

As for the LSWR boat train on that day, it took 4 hours 24 minutes. In general the LSWR could not compete on speed despite its shorter run, but it kept trying and, unlike the GWR, was prepared to take risks. It all ended in July 1906 when the LSWR boat express, rushing over the Salisbury curve, derailed with heavy loss of life. This put an end to railway racing. In the end, the GWR operated the Plymouth boat trains for passengers as well as mail, and built some very fine saloon coaches which remained in service until Plymouth lost its role as a transatlantic port.

The LSWR could afford to lose the battle for prestige with the Plymouth boat trains, since it had won so handsomely with its investment in Southampton Docks. Boat trains, usually with headboards advertising the shipping company concerned, were run from Waterloo Station down to Southampton Docks not only by the LSWR but also by its successors the Southern Railway and British Railways. The LSWR was also interested in cross-channel shipping, but its neighbours the South Eastern & Chatham and the LBSCR were much more involved in the short sea routes.

The LBSCR developed Newhaven, near Brighton, as its cross-channel port, with steamers plying to Le Havre, where the French Etat Railway took passengers on to Paris. As the sea crossing was long, this route was less attractive to passengers than the SECR's Folkestone and Dover routes, but the LBSCR was able to keep its traffic by providing the best service to western France, and also low fares. A night and a day service were offered, and the route was one of the last on which LBSCR steam locomotives hauled express trains amid spreading inter-war electrification. In fact the 'Brighton Atlantics' were still hauling Newhaven boat trains for British Railways in the 1950s.

But it was the SECR which had the major share of continental traffic, utilising not only the Folkestone and Dover facilities but also, at Sheerness, a port convenient for running steamers to Flushing. The SECR was a railway with a low public reputation for the quality of its train services, and there was a long-standing joke about the man who tried to commit suicide on its tracks, where he tied himself to the rail and died of starvation. But in the early twentieth century the Railway did make an effort with its continental services. A harbour branch was laid at Folkestone which, at the price of awkward train working, including a reversal, enabled trains to halt alongside the ships. Henceforth the Folkestone boat trains called at Folkestone Junction, where a pair of small tank engines would attach themselves to the rear and haul the train down to the harbour.

At Dover, the Admiralty, concerned with German naval power, launched its own dockyard scheme, which more or less forced the Railway to reconstruct its facilities. The resulting Dover Marine Station was a handsome terminus alongside a new quay which was still incomplete when World War I started. Simultaneously, the SECR London-Dover lines received the benefit of long-overdue renovation so that high speeds became safe, if still not entirely comfortable. The class of larger and handsome locomotives known as the 'Wainwright 4-4-0s' had come into service and all this enabled the Railway to offer a much improved service, enhanced by the introduction of new steamers.

The fastest train took 90 minutes from Charing Cross to Dover, and on the eve of the war there were seven SECR continental departures from London.

These included the morning and night mails. Night mail, on Fridays, was the 'P & O Express', which connected with Brindisi and the P & O steamer services to India and Australia and, by carrying several vans of mail, was regarded as a vital part of the British Empire's communication system. The 2.05pm departure had coaches for Folkestone, by which Paris could be reached in less than seven hours, and coaches for Dover, which formed the Ostend Boat Express. There were also two boat trains for the Flushing service, which was being transferred from Sheerness to Folkestone because the Great Eastern Railway's service from Harwich had made the long sea trip from Sheerness seem unattractive.

World War I brought this renaissance to an end. Dover Marine, finished in 1915, became a vital part of the British military effort in France, handling hundreds of troop and ambulance trains. In a typical day, six ambulance trains were despatched from Dover and connected with the two or three hospital ships which tied up each day. Operations were not helped by a landslide which blocked the Folkestone-Dover line from late 1915 to the end of the War, but luckily an alternative route through Canterbury was available.

In the brief period between the end of the War and the Railway Amalgamation, the SECR developed the Wainwright 4-4-0s to produce a somewhat more powerful engine in time for the heavier boat trains that appeared in 1921. For the SECR, whose coaching standards had never been especially high, these were quite an innovation, and brought the Railway within sight of the levels witnessed on other companies for decades. Ordinary passengers, which on these trains meant first-

ABOVE: *The 'Dunkirk spirit' lives on in 1955 as passengers queue submissively to join the 'Golden Arrow' at London Victoria.*

RIGHT: William Shakespeare, *a 'Britannia' Pacific, with the 'Golden Arrow' near Folkestone in 1952.*

and second-class passengers who had not paid a supplement to travel Pullman, were provided with corridor coaches for the first time, and third-class passengers had to travel in older coaches tacked on to the rear. All in all, the new boat trains presented a strange, heterogeneous picture, with Pullman cars, the new coaches, and old third-class carriages with their 'bird-cage' roof projections giving the guard a view over the top of the train. Only the colour, crimson lake, was uniform, for even the Pullmans on the SECR had to carry the Railway's colours. The new coaches had end doors only, still a rarity in Britain, and the compartments had removable tables enabling light meals to be served down the train by the Pullman car waiters. For compatibility they also had Pullman-style vestibules and buckeye couplings. For the SECR, which ran the most ramshackle trains to its other coastal resorts like Margate and Ramsgate, these trains were surprisingly adequate.

After the Southern Railway had absorbed the SECR, the continental services were further developed by the introduction of the Pullman 'Golden Arrow' and the 'Night Ferry', but the ordinary boat trains never really impressed their passengers. 4-4-0s continued to be used on these trains even when weights increased, but were relieved by 'King Arthur 4-6-0s' and, later, by the 'West Country' Pacifics.

DOVER-DUNKERQUE-PARIS TRAIN GOING ABOARD THE NIGHT FERRY

ABOVE: *Although the SR and LNER were the main beneficiaries, all four of the railway companies cooperated in publicising continental rail travel. This is one of several posters resulting from this cooperation.*

LEFT: *The 'Night Ferry', bound for Dunkirk and Paris, goes aboard the train ferry at Dover.*

RIGHT: *A 'Merchant Navy' Pacific heads the 'Night Ferry' at London Victoria in the 1950s.*

BOAT TRAINS

On Britain's east coast, almost as much as on the west coast, several ports attempted to develop their passenger traffic, and were helped and encouraged by the local railway companies. Before 1914, the two biggest of the English regional railways not based in London were drawn into this struggle when Hull acquired a steamer link with Zeebrugge. The Lancashire & Yorkshire and the North Eastern railways not only jointly owned the steamer, but also operated a boat train which, by the time it arrived at the quayside, included through coaches from Glasgow, Newcastle, York, Liverpool and Manchester.

The Great Eastern Railway, whose ordinary passenger services were not of high repute, saved its reputation by operating some of the best boat trains in the country. At Parkeston Quay, near Harwich, it served its own and other company's ships to Holland, Germany and Scandinavia. Of these, the Harwich-Hook of Holland route was by far the most important, and provided among other things the fastest transit to northern Germany. In 1904 the GER introduced a specially-built corridor train for the Hook of Holland connection, with an exemplary provision of dining facilities. Over the 69 miles from London this train was timed at 85 minutes, despite its weight and the need to negotiate the Harwich branch. It was a little less than 300 tons with its nine bogie coaches and four smaller vehicles.

In the years preceding World War I, the Great Eastern's 1500 class of inside cylinder 4-6-0 took these trains which, with their weight, faced a gruelling test in the tightly scheduled ascent of the Brentwood Bank, in the London suburbs. After the LNER was formed it built the 'Sandringham' 3-cylinder 4-6-0 locomotives to replace the 4-6-0s of the former Great Central and Great Eastern railways and some of these were allocated to the boat trains. But the GER 4-6-0s were still in service when the new 1924 Hook boat train was introduced. This was of standard LNER design, but included some Pullman cars, and its thirteen bogie vehicles of about 450 tons had to be moved from London to Harwich at an average speed of 50mph. In 1936 yet another train was built for this service, which by this time was officially titled the 'Hook Continental'. This was around 500 tons and, in the old tradition, included good dining car provision with a kitchen car flanked by a first-class diner and a second-class diner. (Boat trains were the last services in Britain to offer second-class accommodation.) As the outward train left London at 8.30pm and the inbound train left Parkeston Quay soon after 6am, dinner and breakfast service was very much appreciated by passengers.

In 1927 business had been increased when the Zeeland Shipping Company, operating to Flushing, which had once used Sheerness, then transferred to Folkestone and decided to make Harwich its terminus. There was also a Danish company operating to Esbjerg, and a steamship line to Antwerp. So apart from the pride of the line, the 'Hook Continental', there were also the 'Antwerp Continental', the 'Flushing Continental', and the 'Scandinavian'. For the day sailing from Harwich to Hook of Holland, the 'Day Continental' was operated.

After World War II most of these services reappeared, although they tended to be hauled less by the 'Sandringhams' than by the new B1 mixed traffic 4-6-0 and, on the heaviest turns, the BR 'Britannia' class of 4-6-2. But even with the latter the timing was 90 minutes. The 'Hook Continental' for a time included coaches of the pre-war LNER streamliners, including first-class armchair coaches. With this accommodation and with the same old tradition of lavish dining facilities, it was in the same league as the 'Golden Arrow'. With the virtual end of transoceanic ship travel and the building of the Channel Tunnel, the modern equivalents of the 'Hook Continental' and of the 'Irish Mail' are expected to be the last of the traditional boat trains to survive.

RIGHT: *One of the LNER's Harwich boat trains arriving at Parkeston Quay in 1934, shortly after the quay's extension. The locomotive is a former Great Eastern 4-6-0, shortly to be replaced on these services by new 'Sandringham' class locomotives.*

BELOW: Doncaster Rovers, *one of the 'Sandringham' 4-6-0 locomotives used by the LNER for Harwich boat trains and other East Anglian services. This picture shows the locomotive in charge of a 'Cambridge Buffet Express', known to successive generations of undergraduates as the 'Beer Train'.*

BELOW, RIGHT: *Another of the 'Sandringham' class in East Anglia. There were more that 70 units in this class, and many were named after football teams in LNER territory. This is* Liverpool.

THE QUEST FOR COMFORT

LEFT: *Return to peacetime normality; passengers board the restored 'Bournemouth Belle' at London Waterloo in 1946.*

With some exceptions in southeastern England and parts of Scotland, the British railways at the turn of the century set themselves a high standard of comfort for passengers on their best trains. Whereas in the United States extra luxury was provided by private rolling stock companies, of which Pullman was the dominant operator, and in Europe by Wagons-Lits, in Britain it was usually the companies themselves which designed and operated luxury rolling stock. There were, however, exceptions to this general rule, for both Pullman and Wagons-Lits did find a place on a few routes.

James Allport of the Midland Railway visited the United States in 1872 and was much impressed by the Pullman operation. Pullman built luxury sleeping and dining cars, staffed them, and had them attached to regular long-distance trains, making money by charging their users a supplementary fare. George Pullman was invited to the next MR shareholders' meeting, where he made proposals which resulted in an agreement whereby the Pullman Company would supply dining, sleeping, and lounge ('parlor') cars and, unusually, vehicles of the same outward form but providing supplement-free ordinary accommodation, as Allport wanted his new train to have a homogeneous profile.

Built in Detroit, re-assembled in Derby, the wooden-built Pullman cars with their clerestory roofs, open iron-railed verandas, and massive bogies made a great impression when the MR staged a press run in early 1874. The sleeping cars had the typical Pullman layout, with lower berths converting to seats for day use while the upper berths were folded up to the roof. They had separate male and female toilets and also provided a stateroom for the really well-to-do traveller. The parlor car, as things turned out, was a closer foretaste of future Pullman operations in Britain. Although it had two private rooms its main part consisted of a lounge with 17 rotating and partly reclinable armchairs.

The train was put into regular service between London St Pancras and Bradford, in June 1874, serving as a day train in one direction and as a night train in the other. It offered several novelties: it was the first British train with toilets for all three classes, and it could claim to

Inter-war Pullman trains

Name	Year of introduction	Route	Mileage	Average mph	Railway
Southern Belle	1908	London-Brighton	51	51	SR
Harrogate Pullman	1923	London-Newcastle	268	47	LNER
West Riding Pullman	1925	London-Halifax	201	47	LNER
Queen of Scots	1928	London-Glasgow	451	47	LNER
Golden Arrow	1929	London-Dover	78	49	SR
Yorkshire Pullman	1935	London-Hull	205	59	LNER
Bournemouth Belle	1931	London-Bournemouth	108	54	SR

THE QUEST FOR COMFORT

be the first British train to be reasonably well heated, as each vehicle had its own coke-fired boiler to supply its radiators.

Interestingly, the non-supplementary-fare vehicles were never popular and were soon discarded. The reason why passengers should spurn this new standard of comfort was uncertain, but they might have been deterred by the unfamiliar American reversible-back seats. In contrast, the parlor car and sleepers attracted a good clientele, largely businessmen, and the next year the MR introduced a day Pullman service to Liverpool. When the Settle & Carlisle route to Scotland was opened the following year, MR Pullman cars were among its well-publicised attractions.

Meanwhile, the London Brighton & South Coast Railway, with a Pullman car assembled by the MR, was taking the first steps towards becoming the most faithful user of Pullman services. In 1875 this company operated

what it called a drawing-room Pullman in some of its London-Brighton trains. Some years later it introduced a twice-daily return trip on this route with a new four-vehicle Pullman set which it called the 'Pullman Limited Express'. New luxuries were added to the now-familiar armchairs, including a buffet, a ladies boudoir, and a compartment for valets and servants. Technically, the train was advanced in its use of electric lighting, although the massive batteries carried beneath the car floors detracted considerably from the tons per seat ratio. The Company installed a steam generator at Victoria Station in London to charge them.

This train was not at first a commercial success. Some potential travellers, so incensed that the train also ran on Sundays, deliberately refrained from using it at all. Moreover, as was the case with other Pullman services, British passengers did not take kindly to the concept of supplementary fares. For a time, the LBSCR withdrew the Sunday service and added non-Pullman first-class stock to the weekday services, and it was not until 1888 that the Company re-introduced Sunday Pullman services, in the form of a Sundays-only train, the 'Sunday Pullman Limited'. This was composed of newly-imported vehicles, the first in Britain to have the Pullman vestibules which made movement from vehicle to vehicle so easy. They were also equipped with a luggage car in which the LBSCR's locomotive engineer had rigged up a generator driven by an axle-driven belt.

This train, virtually a regular excursion train, was popular and so in 1899 became an all-the-year-round service. In 1907, the British Pullman Car Company was bought by the chairman of the Wagons-Lits company, who immediately sought to expand its activities. The first result of this new energy was the transformation of the Brighton 'Sunday Pullman Limited', which was re-equipped and placed on a seven-days-a-week schedule. Seven new cars on 6-axle bogies were built for it, and it was renamed 'Southern Belle'. On weekdays it made two return trips, and on Sundays three, but its speed, typically enough for the LBSCR, was unexciting. At the turn of the century 60 minutes had been allowed for the 51-mile run and although in 1903 there had been a trial in

which the 4-4-0 *Holyrood* had done the trip inside 49 minutes with a maximum speed of 90mph, the new 'Southern Belle' was in motion for precisely four hours per day, exactly the same timing as before. Its moderate pace had the advantage in that several types of locomotive were capable of keeping time with it, not only the new 4-4-2 engines but also the older 4-4-0 machines.

The LBSCR in general refrained from allowing third-class passengers to travel on its better trains, but an exception was made in the case of the midday run of the 'Southern Belle', when patronage would otherwise have been meagre. After the LBSCR had become part of the Southern Railway, the SR decided that all runs of the train should include third-class Pullmans, that is, third-class passengers could use the train on payment of the Pullman supplement. This proved popular, so the train grew to eleven or more Pullman cars, amounting to about 400 tons, and in its last steam-hauled years it was usually hauled by a 'King Arthur' 4-6-0 or one of the big tank engines built by the LBSCR in its last years. The 60-minute schedule was still in force, and was reduced to 55 minutes only in 1967, long after the introduction of the 'Southern Belle's' successor, the 'Brighton Belle', and the electrification of the route.

Elsewhere in southern England, both the London &

THE QUEST FOR COMFORT

LEFT: *The 'Thanet Belle', introduced by the Southern Railway between London and Ramsgate. The locomotive is of the 'Battle of Britain' class, which was identical with the 'West Countrys'. This locomotive, probably provided especially for this inaugural photograph, is named* Manston, *commemorating Ramsgate's celebrated RAF base.*

LOWER, LEFT: *The 'Golden Arrow' on arrival at London Victoria in 1947, hauled by a 'Battle of Britain' locomotive. This was one of the relatively few British locomotive types to be provided with electric headlamps, but an oil rear lamp has had to be added in preparation for backing out from the station.*

BELOW: *Inside the buffet car of the post-war 'Golden Arrow'.*

BOTTOM: *Dover Marine, April 1946; the 'Golden Arrow' is restored after its wartime discontinuance. For the occasion,* Channel Packet, *the first of the 'Merchant Navy' Pacifics, has been provided.*

South Western and the South Eastern & Chatham railways established a tradition of luxury trains in the late nineteenth century. In the days before the fiercely competitive London Chatham & Dover and South Eastern railways agreed to sink their differences and combine in the SECR, luxury service to France was a main battlefield. The London Chatham & Dover began hostilities in 1889, the year of the Paris Exhibition, by running a train of Wagons-Lits vehicles to Dover and providing a new steamer for the Dover-Calais route to connect with another Wagons-Lits train at Calais, which took passengers on to Paris.

This new train, which can be regarded as the forerunner to the later 'Golden Arrow', consisted of four open-plan saloons and two baggage cars. The saloons had armchairs, and meals could be served at passengers' seats from a kitchen in one of the baggage cars. The SER responded immediately to this challenge by ordering its own Wagons-Lits train, with the result that two similar trains, arriving within five minutes of each other at Dover, split the traffic between them. This traffic was not great in any case, probably thanks to the British passengers' dislike of supplementary fares. Both trains were loss-makers, and sometimes did not carry a single revenue passenger. By 1893 they had both been withdrawn.

The SER, however, decided to pursue the luxury-train idea further. It ordered some vehicles from Pullman's American competitor, the Gilbert Car Manufacturing Company. These were re-assembled at Ashford and then presented to the press. The design was certainly luxurious, with a smoking compartment seating seven, and only 17 rotating armchairs in the main saloon. The interiors were American ornate at its most florid. A six-car train was built, with four saloon cars, a buffet car and a baggage car, with ordinary SER brakevans at each end. It was designed for the Hastings-London service, to give the SER a competitive edge over the rival LBSCR; and in order to make the train additionally attractive, only the first-class fare was charged, with no supplement. However, as the passenger per vehicle ratio was so low, the train was an obvious loss-maker and was soon withdrawn and the vehicles were added as singles or pairs to existing London-Dover and London-Hastings trains as an extra attraction. Then, in 1896, the Gilbert cars were rebuilt to form a high-class commuter train on the Hastings-London run.

Meanwhile the SER, despite its difficulties with the Gilbert cars, decided to introduce its own Pullman-style service with vehicles which it ordered in Britain. These formed the 'Folkestone Vestibuled Express', which actually exceeded the extravagances of the Gilbert train with its internal and external decor. It carried third-class passengers too, allowing exceptionally spacious seating, with single seats along one side of the aisle and double seats along the other. The third-class vehicle also had a ladies' section, whereas the second-class vehicles, similar in layout, offered a smoking room instead. The first-class car was an extravagant mix of all possible luxuries with sofas, fixed armchairs, and rotating armchairs. In general, this train made a startling contrast with the generally abysmal standard of SER trains.

When the SER and LCDR became the SECR, the SER's dislike of the Pullman company soon disappeared, as it had been little more than a foible of the SER chairman. Before World War I the Pullman Company, now British-owned in Europe, was operating its cars in the

ABOVE: *The Pullman car* Minerva *receives special attention at the Battersea yards in 1938, in preparation for use by the King and Queen on the occasion of a royal visit to Paris. It was traditional for Pullman cars to be individually named.*

LEFT: *The interior of a 1930s Wagons-Lits dining car, used in continental service. Wagons-Lits had a very minor role in Britain. But it was strong in western Europe, dominating the dining and sleeping car services of several railway systems, including that of France.*

ABOVE: *The 'Bournemouth Belle' awaits departure from London Waterloo in 1939.* Sir Pelleas, *of the 'King Arthur' class, is in charge. These two-cylinder 4-6-0 engines, based on a LSWR design, were built in several varieties by the Southern Railway.* Sir Pelleas *belonged to a group introduced in 1925. All bore names of characters from the King Arthur legends.*

Dover and Folkestone boat trains. After the War, the Gilbert cars and those of the 'Folkstone Vestibuled Express' were rebuilt by Pullman, and in 1921 the 'Thanet Pullman Limited' was introduced as a Sundays-only high-class excursion train from London to Margate and Ramsgate. Being a Sunday train, one of the newer E1 class 4-4-0 locomotives was available to haul it on its fast schedule of 90 minutes for the 74-miles London-Margate run. However, patronage of this train did not at all correspond with its high running costs, and consequently, by 1931 the new Southern Railway was running the train with ordinary rolling stock and a single Pullman car. In 1948, after wartime suspension, a replacement for this train was introduced, the 'Thanet Belle' (later 'Kentish Belle'), which comprised two first-class and eight third-class Pullman vehicles. On weekdays, it left London in the morning, but on Saturdays and Sundays, departure was in the afternoon and in both cases returned from Ramsgate in the early evening. Later, the train operated two return services on Saturdays, the day of heaviest demand. In retrospect, with the short distances involved it seems likely that in southeast England these expensive trains could only have become commercially viable if they had made two return trips daily.

The culmination of the luxury train in Kent was the 'Golden Arrow', successor in 1929 to the old-established 'Calais Boat Express', which departed at 11am from London Victoria. In fact, the new all-Pullman boat train had been running between London and Dover since 1924, but the full 'Golden Arrow' service was not inaugurated until five years later. It then consisted of the British train, a new cross-channel steamer, the *Canterbury*, and the corresponding French Pullman train, the 'Flèche d'Or' ('Golden Arrow').

A feature of the new service was that passengers could register their baggage at departure, and it was then taken to London or Paris in special containers, to undergo customs examination on arrival rather than in the uncongenial halls of Calais and Dover. 'Golden Arrow' passengers were also scheduled to arrive at the quayside several minutes before the ordinary boat train and so saved from that other anxiety of cross-channel ports, not finding a good place on the boat. In addition, a special bus was operated from Kings Cross Station in London to connect with Pullman trains serving the north of Britain, making it possible to travel by Pullman all the way from the Scottish to the French capital.

The Pullman cars for both the French and British 'Golden Arrow' trains were built in Britain so that the trains on both sides of the Channel should match perfectly. Initially they were painted in umber and cream, but when the Depression led to the French train taking second-class Pullman cars as well, its livery was changed

LEFT: *A Pullman conductor uses the latest technology to issue a supplementary fare ticket aboard the 'Bournemouth Belle' in 1946.*

RIGHT: *The inaugural post-war run of the 'Bournemouth Belle'; the fireman makes sure that the smokebox is airtight.*

BELOW: *The 'Bournemouth Belle' in 1955, hauled by* Brocklebank Line *of the 'Merchant Navy' class.*

to dark blue and cream. The familiar brass table lamps, almost a trademark of Pullman in Britain, and the upholstery and internal panelling, remained identical in the British and French trains.

The time of transfer from train to ship was scheduled to take only 17 minutes, which helped to bring the London-Paris transit time down to 6½ hours. With the allowance of 1 hour 38 minutes for the London-Dover run, which implied an average speed of almost 50mph, and the 12-car load, the demand on the locomotive was quite heavy, and for many years the Southern Railway used its biggest passenger engines, the 'Lord Nelson' class, for this train. Even when the Pullman cars were reduced to four, supplemented by six ordinary coaches, the train was still only 50 tons less than the 425-ton maximum allowed for one engine up the climbs to Knockholt and to Sevenoaks Tunnel. A curiosity of the inter-war 'Golden Arrow' was that the southbound service was via Dover, but the inbound service was via Folkestone. In both cases, an average speed of 60mph was demanded over the straight track between the towns of Tonbridge and Folkestone.

After the War the 'Golden Arrow' was reinstated as

early as 1946, by which time the Southern Railway's air-smoothed 4-6-2s of the 'Merchant Navy' and 'West Country' classes were available to haul it. For a time, too, the BR 4-6-2 *William Shakespeare* was regularly turned out for this train. The locomotives were decorated with gilt arrows on their sides and on their smokebox doors, with a round headboard and French and British flags at the front.

Because port formalities took longer in the post-war years, the London-Paris timing deteriorated to almost seven hours despite some electrification on both sides of the Channel. Steam haulage in Britain of this train ceased in 1962, but continued a few years longer between Calais and Amiens. Declining patronage and growing numbers of non-Pullman passengers prompted the French Railways to withdraw the Pullman cars, and this was eventually followed by the withdrawal of the British 'Golden Arrow' in 1972.

Another distinguished boat service through Dover was the 'Night Ferry', the only Wagons-Lits service to run in Britain in the twentieth century, and also the only passenger service in Britain to use a train ferry. Train ferries, the precursor of modern roll-on, roll-off ferries,

had been tried in Britain during World War I, when they were used to take trainloads of supplies to the British army in France. In 1924, a freight-only train ferry had been established between Harwich and Zeebrugge. This was successful, despite the awkwardness imposed by British railways' dimensional restrictions; and continental railways wishing to despatch freightcars to British destinations used special, scaled-down, rolling stock.

It was not until 1936 that the passenger 'Night Ferry' service was established, with the train using a new train ferry between Dover and Dunkirk. It was not intended to provide a fast London-Paris service, but one which would enable the passenger to travel overnight between the two capitals without losing any sleep. Blue Wagons-Lits sleeping cars and baggage cars ran between the two terminals, but non-sleeper first- and second-class passengers were provided with accommodation in ordinary stock and also had to make their own way between train and boat at Dover and Dunkirk. The Wagons-Lits passengers travelled in luxury and, provided they were not disturbed by the shunting on and off the train ferry, had a good night's sleep.

At its peak, the 'Night Ferry' included ten sleeping cars, plus the baggage cars, which went all the way, together with seven Southern Railway vehicles attached or detached at Dover to provide sitting accommodation and dining facilities. The Wagons-Lits cars had been specially built, and were narrower and shorter than standard continental cars. Although the timing between London and Dover was a little lower than that of the other boat trains, the weight of this train necessitated the use of two locomotives, two 4-4-0s of SECR vintage being typically used before the War. For a short time after the War, a single 'West Country' 4-6-2 was sufficient, but in the course of time it was found necessary to pilot this with one of the 4-4-0s. Towards the end of the steam era, the larger 'Merchant Navy' and 'Britannia' 4-6-2s were used. Electric traction took over in 1959, and the train was finally withdrawn in 1980, on the grounds that its future traffic did not justify building new stock to replace the 1936 vehicles. In its last years, passenger appeal had fallen off, partly because of competition with air travel and, later, by the withdrawal of dining facilities, the loss of which meant that it could no longer be regarded as a luxury train. To make up for lost passengers, from 1957 it carried vehicles destined for Brussels in addition to the Paris cars, but these were not enough to reverse its declining fortunes.

Elsewhere in southern England, the London & South Western Railway in the 1880s provided a Pullman

one of the lighter 'West Country' Pacifics. The 'Devon Belle' was notable for its observation car, which Pullman provided by rebuilding old third-class cars. After its initial popularity, the 'Devon Belle' began to lose patronage. possibly because the kind of people who used it were among the first to abandon railway transport in favour of their own cars. After the 1954 summer season the train was dropped from the timetables.

The GWR had never been keen on the Pullman concept, believing that distances in Britain were too short to make luxury accommodation necessary and preferring, in the exceptional cases, to provide its own facilities. It did build some Pullman-style saloons for its Plymouth boat train, but in 1929 experienced a short-lived Pullman enthusiasm. It placed a genuine Pullman car in its boat train, and also introduced the all-Pullman 'Torquay Pullman'. Neither of these innovations proved commercially successful, although it could be argued that the GWR hardly gave them a chance, for it withdrew them in 1930, the Pullman Company thereupon using the rolling stock for the Southern Railway's boat trains and 'Bournemouth Belle'. That was the end of the GWR's interest in Pullman service but its successor, the Western Region of BR, introduced the 'South Wales Pullman' in 1955. This was an eight-car formation of rather elderly Pullman stock, invariably hauled by a 'Castle' 4-6-0, which made the London-Swansea trip in 3 hours 55 minutes. It was successful enough to pave the way for the diesel 'South Wales Pullman' of 1961.

Despite its energetic salesmanship, the Pullman Company did not attract the interest of many companies. A late exception was the Caledonian Railway which, in 1914, contracted Pullman to provide dining and buffet cars for its best services and also for *Maid of Morven*, the first observation car to run in Britain. Intended for the scenic Glasgow-Oban line, it was distinguished by its vast expanse of window.

Sometimes high-powered salesmanship would result in a railway company regretting a new contract it had signed with Pullman. This happened with the Great Central Railway in 1909, which signed a 15-year agreement to operate all-Pullman trains. The contract was unusual in that Pullman was to gain its revenue not by charging supplementary fares but by taking ten percent of the trains' gross revenues. A few months after the agreement, the GCR disowned it.

A few years later the American manager of the Great Eastern Railway, a Pullman enthusiast, contracted for a large number of cars for the best East Anglian expresses. When the GER's successor, the London & North Eastern Railway, discovered that it was saddled with this contract, it decided to use a few of the vehicles for its Harwich boat trains, and to find more promising routes for the others, as it did not regard East Anglia as likely Pullman territory. It introduced in 1923 its 'Harrogate Pullman' and then, impressed by the success of the latter, began to operate its 'Sheffield Pullman', which used the old Great Northern route as far as Nottingham, and thence the Great Central line up to Sheffield. But not even Sheffield and Nottingham combined could provide a revenue load for this five-car train. It was then decided to change the route so that Nottingham was omitted but Manchester added as the terminal station. But the 'Sheffield and Manchester Pullman' likewise failed to attract a substantial clientele. It then became a London-Leeds-Bradford Pullman train, which in 1928 became the 'West Riding Pullman' and seven years later was renamed the

LEFT, TOP: *A 1947 photograph purporting to show holidaymakers enjoying the conviviality of the 'Devon Belle's' observation car. The alleged passengers are probably Southern Railway office staff mobilised for the occasion.*

LEFT: *An exterior view of the 'Devon Belle' observation car. Such cars, unlike in North America, were very rare in Britain. They differed from most American observation cars in that they were not restricted to first class passengers.*

ABOVE: *The 'South Wales Pullman' on arrival at Swansea. The rolling stock was already archaic in the 1950s, when this photograph was taken, but was nevertheless comfortable inside.*

service, but not a complete Pullman train, on its London-Plymouth line, presumably to give it a competitive edge over the GWR. Although this venture was not a success, in the next decade another experimental Pullman service, this time to Bournemouth, developed well, with four of the Bournemouth trains provided with a Pullman drawing room car in both directions. But in 1905, the LSWR built new corridor trains, with restaurant cars, for this line, and the advance was considered sufficient to make Pullman service redundant.

However, in 1931, the LSWR's successor, the Southern Railway, introduced its 'Bournemouth Belle', a Sundays-only service on this route, which became a daily service five years later. Usually, this train comprised seven Pullman cars in winter and ten in the summer, of which two were first-class and the others third-class. As some of the vehicles were large twelve-wheelers, the train could weigh up to 400 tons at peak periods and was almost always hauled by one of the 'Lord Nelson' 4-6-0s, the same engine being used in both directions. The train had intermediate stops at Bournemouth West and Southampton, but ran the 79 miles from Southampton to London in 85 minutes, which meant that the full trip took just two hours for the 111 miles.

After the wartime withdrawal of Pullmans, the train was reinstated in 1946 and, with 'Merchant Navy' Pacifics now available, sometimes weighed as much as 550 tons which, with the long 1 in 250 gradient through Winchester, was a hard test for those locomotives. The 'Merchant Navy' class was also used on a new Pullman train introduced in 1947, the 'Devon Belle', from London to Plymouth and Ilfracombe. This train could comprise as many as 14 vehicles at summer weekends, and likewise gave the new Pacifics a chance to show what they could do. Advertised as non-stop between London and Exeter, the train in fact stopped just past Salisbury to change engines. At Exeter, the Plymouth and Ilfracombe sections were separated, with each going forward behind

'Yorkshire Pullman' with extension to Hull. This extension was accompanied by a rescheduling, which included a 60mph average over the 156 miles between London and Doncaster. In the last pre-war years it was typically an eight-car formation, although at peaks it was enlarged sometimes to twelve cars. Gresley's Pacifics were the favoured motive power, although the mixed traffic V2 2-6-2s also showed that they could handle it. It was reinstated after the War, but on a slower schedule, and was dieselised in 1961.

As for the LNER's other Pullman venture, the 'Harrogate Pullman', this was a success right from the start. Harrogate Spa, as it preferred to call itself, was becoming a fashionable resort and this luxury train precisely answered the needs of its clientele. It was rescheduled from time to time, as initially it served Leeds on the exceptionally fast timing of 3 hours 25 minutes from London, but after the introduction of the 'West Riding Pullman' the Leeds stop was omitted. It initially consisted of two first-class and two second-class Pullman cars, hauled by a GCR 'Director' 4-4-0 locomotive, but it was not long before Great Northern Atlantics became the regular tractive power.

Despite its name, the 'Harrogate Pullman' actually continued beyond that resort to Newcastle and then, from 1925, to Edinburgh. In 1928 it was re-equipped with the first all-steel Pullman cars to run in Britain, and was renamed, logically enough, as the 'Queen of Scots'.

Although it took three quarters of an hour longer than the 'Flying Scotsman' to reach Edinburgh, it attracted a sizable sector of the Anglo-Scottish traffic, as it was the most comfortable service available. Later, it was extended to Glasgow. Before its withdrawal in 1939 the Gresley Pacifics were beginning to take over from the Atlantics, but after the train's reinstatement in 1952, it was usually hauled by one of the 1946-design Pacifics. It continued running up to 1964, when it was cut back to Harrogate, and for a few more years ran under the name of the 'White Rose'.

British Rail introduced a new all-Pullman train to the East Coast route in 1948. This was the London-Newcastle 'Tees-Tyne Pullman', an eight-car train which because of its popularity with northeastern businessmen soon became a nine-car formation which included a bar car. It survived into the diesel era, but BR in due course became disenchanted with the Pullman concept and withdrew Pullman services, only to change its mind a few years later. After a hundred years there were still passengers who were willing to pay extra for the Pullman service. The general ambience of the cars, the personal service by Pullman attendants, the familiar white tablecloths and comfortable chairs, the brass lamps, the meals served at the passenger's own table from kitchen cars distributed down the train, all these made Pullman travel something of an experience in pampering, a far-from-pale imitation of life on ocean liners.

RIGHT: *The 'Queen of Scots' Pullman train in the 1930s.*

BELOW: *Old Pullman cars, no longer required for regular use, found a ready market. Some were used for steam excursions, while other vehicles were assembled to form the vintage 'Orient Express' tourist train. This picture shows* Flying Scotsman *hauling Pullman cars making up the 'Cumbrian Mountain Pullman' in 1983.*

RIGHT, BELOW: *Another 1983 steam excursion using Pullman cars, on this occasion hauled by an LNER 2-6-0.*

THE RACE
TO THE
NORTH
RENEWED

LEFT: *The LNER Pacific* Papyrus *leaves London Kings Cross on its record-breaking run of 5 March 1935.*

When the railways amalgamated, the companies formerly belonging to the West Coast consortium became part of the new LMS, which in turn included the two companies that formed the Midland Railway's Anglo-Scottish route. The East Coast consortium became part of the LNER. Each of the three routes were henceforth under integrated managements, but during the 1920s there was little sign of the old inter-company competition. The LNER and LMS still observed the informal agreement where day trains between London and Edinburgh or Glasgow should not be scheduled at less than 8¼ hours. Other, unwritten, agreements also existed. For example, a burst of competitive scheduling in 1910 had pitted the GNR against the MR for the London-Leeds traffic, but this had ended with an agreement on minimum schedules which the new companies continued to observe.

If there had been a race between London and Scotland, the LNER would have been best-placed. The LMS locomotive department was firmly tied to Midland practice and until 1927 had no really adequate locomotives for the heavy, fast, long-distance hauls. Then, its impatient management decided to order a new class of 3-cylinder 4-6-0 from an outside builder. This was the 'Royal Scot' class, which was capable of good performance but, until it was radically rebuilt in the 1940s, was not an outstanding design. Meanwhile the LNER was building further examples of the Gresley Pacific that had been designed originally for the GNR. This, too, was a capable engine but, weight for weight, was not as good as its predecessor, the GNR Atlantic. However, Gresley persevered and after some modification this class A1, of which *Flying Scotsman* became the best-known member, proved to be an outstanding design in terms of speed and horsepower. When Gresley modified the design to create class A3, with a higher boiler pressure, it was evident that the LNER had a winner.

Some of the LNER Pacifics had a tender with its own corridor, enabling enginemen to be relieved without stopping the train. With this facility, in 1928 the LNER introduced regular non-stop running between London and Edinburgh. The immediate response to this by the LMS showed that rivalry still existed between the East and West coast routes; the LMS with appropriate publicity, and on one day only, also ran a train non-stop from London to Scotland. As the LMS London-Glasgow route was 401 miles, and the LNER's London-Edinburgh run only 393, the LMS could claim to have achieved the longest non-stop run, a steam record which lasted for twenty years.

There was one alleged 'race to the north' in 1928. This was between the LNER and Imperial Airways. The latter, in need of publicity, arranged an amicable demonstration in which its three-engined biplane carrying 21 passengers would leave London at the same time as the 'Flying Scotsman', would rendezvous with the train as the latter crossed the Tweed by the Royal Border Bridge, and then proceed to Edinburgh. This was not a race, it was stressed, but would show that airliners were capable of flying over such long routes. In the event, with its fuel stops and somewhat longer route along the coastline the airliner lagged behind the 'Flying Scotsman', and rendezvoused with the wrong train at the Tweed. Its passengers arrived at Edinburgh's Waverley Station by taxi from the airport some minutes after the 'Flying Scotsman' had arrived but, interestingly enough, many newspapers claimed that there had indeed been a race

The dimensions of the East and West Coast Pacifics

Type	Year	Cylinders (ins)	Coupled wheel diameter	Grate area (sq ft)	Boiler pressure (psi)	Tractive effort (lbs)	Weight on coupled wheels (tons)
LNER							
A3	1927	(3) 19×26	6ft 8in	41	220	32,900	66
A4	1935	(3) 18×26	6ft 8in	41	250	35,500	66
MS							
Princess							
Elizabeth	1933	(4) 16×28	6ft 6in	45	250	40,300	67
Coronation	1937	(4) 16×28	6ft 9in	50	250	40,000	67

(The bigger grates of the LMS engines, facing heavier gradients, is a key difference.)

Longest British non-stop runs in 1939

Railway	Departure Station	Arrival Station	Mileage	Time	Average mph
LNER	London	Edinburgh	393	7h 0m	56
LMS	London	Carlisle	299	4h 43m	63
LNER	Newcastle	London	268	3h 57m	68
LMS	Glasgow	Crewe	243	5h 5m	48
LNER	London	Darlington	232	3h 18m	70
GWR	London	Plymouth	226	4h 0m	56

THE RACE TO THE NORTH RENEWED

and that Imperial Airways had won. This inaccuracy might be regarded as characteristic of the British press, but it did show that the newspapers had a thirst for sensations likes races to the north.

This thirst was satisfied by the renewal of competitive scheduling between the East Coast and West Coast routes that occurred in the 1930s. In the USA and Germany, diesel-powered trains were setting new speed records and the LNER was particularly interested in the German 'Flying Hamburger', whose manufacturers were invited to submit proposals for a similar train to run between London and Newcastle, and London and Leeds. However, despite their somewhat cramped passenger accommodation, the proposed trains could not offer an appreciably improved schedule. Gresley had been among those who had pursued this proposal, but his disappointment was diverted when the LNER management suggested that his Pacifics, hauling standard rolling stock, could probably do better than the German diesel railcars.

Some experimental runs were then organised. A four-vehicle train hauled by the A1 Pacific *Flying Scotsman* ran from London to Leeds at an average speed of 73mph, reaching 95mph on one stretch. The following year, 1935, a six-car train was run from London to Newcastle and back behind *Papyrus*, one of the A3 Pacifics with higher boiler pressure. Northbound, an average of 70mph was achieved, with the highest speed about 88mph. The relatively small difference between the maximum and the average speeds showed that this performance was achieved by a locomotive working normally, without any special effort being made to break records. On the southbound trip, however, an attempt was made on the world record. Descending Stoke Bank, perhaps the most suitable location in Britain for a high-speed run, *Papyrus* averaged 100mph over twelve miles and reached a maximum of 108mph, which was a world record. Out and back, the locomotive had run 300 miles at over 80mph.

LEFT: *On the footplate of a GN Atlantic, predecessor of the LNER Pacifics.*

ABOVE: *The LMS Royal Scot locomotive is loaded aboard at Tilbury Docks, en route for the Chicago World Fair of 1933.*

RIGHT: Royal Scot *on tour in North America.*

NEXT PAGE: *Best-known of the LNER Pacifics, and now preserved; Flying Scotsman with a steam excursion in 1986.*

This run was the prelude to the introduction of the new fast 'Silver Jubilee' service between London and Newcastle. But although the A3 Pacifics, which were still being built, seemed capable of coping with the task, Gresley decided that the design could be usefully modified to produce a Pacific of even better high-speed capability. A higher boiler pressure (250 instead of 220 psi), slightly smaller cylinders, and more generous internal steam passages to prevent 'throttling' of the steam at high speeds, were the main changes, but Gresley was also persuaded to fit streamlined casings around the new locomotives.

The first of the new streamlined Pacifics, Class A4, was *Silver Link*, which hauled the new 'Silver Jubilee' train on a trial run in September 1935. On the northbound run the first 76 miles to Peterborough were covered at an average of 83mph, with 112mph being reached on two occasions. This performance seemed almost effortless, achieved with an economy of steam that suggested that 80mph averages were close to the optimum point of the speed range for this design. The new 'Silver Jubilee' train set was of 230 tons, slightly more than the 215 tons handled by *Papyrus*.

The 'Silver Jubilee', Britain's first streamlined train, went into regular service at the end of the month. It left Newcastle at 10.00am, stopped at Darlington, and then did the remaining 232 miles to London at an average of 70mph. It arrived in London at 2pm, and went back at 5.30pm, again offering a 4-hour schedule. The operation of such high-speed trains required several innovations. Two block sections were kept clear ahead of the train, instead of the one block maintained for normal trains. Also, because the engines were so free-running, it was felt

that drivers should have speed indicators so as to avoid accidental infringements of speed restrictions. These were of the recording type, and their tapes were examined anxiously in the first months of the service to detect any cases where speed might have been dangerously high. But in fact, like their A3 predecessors, these Pacifics showed that they could maintain tight schedules, not by successive bursts of exceptionally high speed but by consistent high-speed running for mile after mile.

Four A4 locomotives were initially built for this service. Like the coaches, they were painted silver-grey with stainless-steel fittings, and their names all began with 'Silver'. The train was of seven coaches, of which six were articulated twin-sets, so that only ten bogies carried the whole train, which weighed barely 200 tons. Later, because of its popularity, the train was enlarged by replacing the odd seventh coach with an additional twin-set. Despite the supplementary fare that was charged, the train frequently ran with every one of its first- and third-class seats occupied. That supplementary fare, it was later said, returned the capital cost of the train within two years.

Up to this point, while the LMS had watched with some unhappiness the speed exploits of the LNER, and also of the GWR's 'Cheltenham Flyer', its worries had been in terms of publicity rather than of commerce. But the LNER decided that London-Edinburgh would be the best route on which to repeat the success of the 'Silver Jubilee'. In 1937, with a burst of the publicity in which the LNER had become so expert, it was announced that two new fast luxury trains would be introduced. One would be the 'Coronation' from London to Edinburgh, and the other a London to Leeds service operating according to

ABOVE: *A rare picture of* Great Northern, *the pioneer Gresley Pacific. This locomotive was later rebuilt as a prototype of a new, post-Gresley, class of Pacific.*

RIGHT, TOP: Flying Scotsman *in excursion service, here led by another preserved LNER locomotive,* Mayflower.

RIGHT: *The record-breaking* Papyrus. *This is a post-war picture which shows the double chimney fitted to several members of this class to enhance steam production.*

LEFT: *The Kings Cross stationmaster views the insignia of the new* Silver Fox, *the fourth of the A4 Pacifics to be built.*

BELOW: *The all-silver 'Silver Jubilee' train leaving London Kings Cross on its trial run of 27 September 1935, during which it reached a new record speed of 112mph, and covered a 41-mile stretch at 100mph. The locomotive is the A4 Pacific* Silver Link.

THE RACE TO THE NORTH RENEWED

RIGHT: *An artist's view of* Silver Link, *hauling the post-war 'Flying Scotsman', picking up water. For a short period, British Railways painted its major passenger locomotives in this shade of blue.*

BELOW: *The preserved LMS Pacific* Princess Elizabeth *at work on a steam excursion in 1976.*

"THE FLYING SCOTSMAN", DRAWN BY "SILVER LINK", PICKING UP
WATER AT SPEED

the schedule achieved by *Flying Scotsman* in its trial run of 1934. Both these routes were competitive with LMS services, and the LMS realised that something would have to be done about it.

Luckily, William Stanier had become Chief Mechanical Engineer of the LMS in 1932. Bringing with him the experience of GWR practice, to which he had made several improvements, he put an end to the disorganised and ineffective locomotive policy hitherto prevailing on the railway, where ex-LNWR and ex-Midland engineers had seemed incapable of venomless co-operation. His first two Pacifics, *Princess Royal* and *Princess Elizabeth*, had been introduced in 1933 and, after trial running, had been joined in 1935 by ten others to a slightly improved design. In some way similar to the GWR 'Kings', these locomotives had more boiler capacity than the latter and were designed for hauling the Anglo-Scottish trains, which were not especially fast but involved the haulage of heavy loads up stiff gradients. Simultaneously, Stanier built large numbers of a new passenger 4-6-0, the 3-cylinder 'Jubilee' class, which replaced the small Midland 4-4-0s on express trains over several main lines and hauled the top trains over lines which could not accept the 'Royal Scots'. One of their duties was to haul the London-Manchester 'Mancunian', which had a 'Royal Scot' in the southbound direction but needed something lighter for its northbound route via Stoke-on-Trent.

When the LMS management heard that the LNER 'Coronation' was to introduce a six-hour schedule be-

tween London and Edinburgh, it immediately began to examine the possibility of a six-hour London-Glasgow schedule over the West Coast Route. Late in 1936 it organised a trial run in which *Princess Elizabeth* was entrusted with a 230-ton train and a six-hour schedule. Meticulous planning went into this effort and it was decided to make it a non-stop run. As the LMS did not use corridor tenders, a third man was added to the engine crew on this occasion.

Despite the dozens of permanent speed restrictions, the speed as far as Carlisle on the outward run averaged 70mph, and to Glasgow, despite the obstacle of Beattock Bank, the average was 68mph, with the entire trip being accomplished in 5 hours 54 minutes. For the return run an extra coach was added, but similar speeds were maintained.

Although *Princess Elizabeth* had performed well, it was decided that the design should be modified for hauling the proposed new trains. The new class of Pacific was streamlined and, like the A4s of the LNER, had enlarged and smoothed internal steam passages. The first locomotive was called *Coronation*, and, in the course of time, 38 units were built; but not all were streamlined, and after World War II the streamlining was removed from those units which had been so fitted. In 1939 *Duchess of Abercorn* of this class achieved a record 3300 indicated horsepower output when hauling a heavy train up Beattock Bank.

In the end, the new LMS Anglo-Scottish train, the

'Coronation Scot', was given a 6½ hour schedule instead of the 6 hour which had been hoped for. Because it was not a new train, but simply replaced the Glasgow section of the old 'Midday Scot', it was hardly on the same level as the LNER's new 'Coronation'. However, the frequent speed restrictions on the West Coast Route would have required frequent sharp braking if a 6-hour schedule had been instituted, and this would have been irritating for passengers. Since the LMS trains were well-filled in any case, the commerical argument for a 6-hour schedule was not strong.

Nevertheless, the LMS did make one effort to steal the LNER's thunder, or at least part of it. After *Coronation* emerged from Crewe Works, it was entrusted with a test train that was quietly intended to beat the 112mph speed record held by the LNER. This train was operated in the guise of a publicity run for the new engine, but it was not handled well, and resulted in the train almost derailing when it traversed the Crewe crossovers at excessive speed, not having had time to properly brake. The LMS announced that 114mph had been reached, although four independent timers on the train agreed that 112½mph had been the maximum.

The next day the LNER made a press-and-publicity run with the new 'Coronation' train from London to just beyond Grantham. Although on the return trip the A4 Pacific was driven very hard, the intention of beating the new claimed LMS speed record was not achieved, as *Dominion of Canada* reached only 109mph.

ABOVE: *The 'Royal Scot' picking up water from Bushey troughs. The locomotive is* Princess Beatrice *of the same class as* Princess Elizabeth. *Only 12 units were built of this class, which had some similarities with the GWR 'Kings'.*

RIGHT: *Another view of* Princess Elizabeth *in excursion service during the 1980s.* Princess Margaret Rose *of this class has also been preserved.*

Five A4s, named after the three dominions, and India and South Africa, were allocated for working the 'Coronation', which went into regular service in July 1937. It was a more difficult proposition than the 'Silver Jubilee', being heavier and longer. The length of the engine's run meant that drivers could not overtax the locomotive without risking the exhaustion of coal supplies *en route*.

The empty weight of the nine coaches was 312 tons, and would have been more had not eight of the vehicles been articulated twins. The last vehicle was a unique vehicle, whose beavertail end gave the rear of the train a wedge shape to match the similar shape of the A4 streamliner at the front. This configuration was expected to reduce the air drag at the rear and suited the purpose of the vehicle, which was an observation car. It was provided with movable armchairs, and passengers could use it by paying one shilling per hour. It was soon decided to remove it during the winter months, because the train left London for the north at 4pm, and from Edinburgh for the south at 4.30pm, which meant that in winter most of the trip was in darkness, when few passengers would see the point of sitting in the observation car.

ABOVE: *The first of the LMS streamlined Pacifics,* Coronation, *is rolled out from the Crewe workshops.*

LEFT, ABOVE: *One of many LNER inter-war posters. The railway companies were valuable clients for contemporary artists.*

LEFT: *A line-up of LNER streamlined locomotives in 1937. Interestingly, the locomotive at the far right is not a Pacific, but No.10000, a 4-6-4 of which only one example was built.*

RIGHT: *An LNER poster advertising the 'Coronation' train to Scotland, emphasising the most scenic part of the trip over the former North British Railway's line between Berwick and Edinburgh, much of it laid along the rugged coastline. The well-known slogan 'It's quicker by rail' was used by all four railway companies over several years.*

BELOW: *Another view of* Coronation's *debut. The oval buffers favoured by the LMS are conspicuous in this picture.*

"THE CORONATION"
ON THE EAST COAST ENTERING SCOTLAND
IT'S QUICKER BY RAIL
FULL INFORMATION FROM ANY L·N·E·R OFFICE OR AGENCY

The 'Coronation' was the finest and most memorable of all British trains, combining an exciting schedule with original rolling stock and a decor which, while plainly of the 1930s, did not carry fashion to the excess of poor taste. The exterior was enamelled, with light blue for the upper panels and a darker blue for the lower, and the allocated engines were painted in the darker shade. The coaches were open-plan, although in first class, each seat was placed in a kind of alcove, which also offered a table, and the chair could be swivelled towards the window. The windows were large, double, and unopenable because this was the first British train to use pressure ventilation, changing the air every three minutes or so.

The interior decor was colourful, even though aluminium was dominant. A great effort was made to overcome noise, with the generous use of acoustic blanketing and attention to other details. Two kitchens enabled meals to be served at passenger's tables, Pullman-style, and the cutlery had flat handles so that it would not rattle.

Supplementary fares were charged, and evidently passengers paid them willingly, because the train remained popular even after the first excitement had worn off. Because of the distance, two train sets had to be provided. During World War II, all the LNER streamlined trains were taken out of service and laid up in a remote location, and none was ever used as a complete train again. After the War the 'Talisman' was introduced in place of the 'Coronation', and it included one of the latter's twin-sets, although this was inferior to its predecessor.

The third LNER streamliner was the 'West Riding Limited', which began operations in September 1937. This linked London with Leeds and Bradford and used a

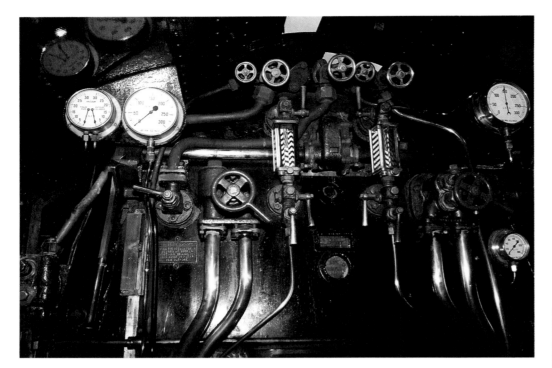

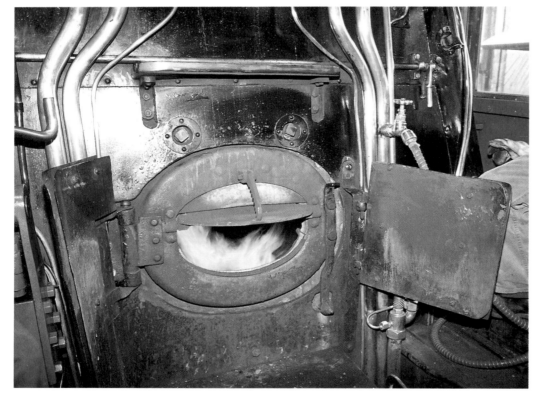

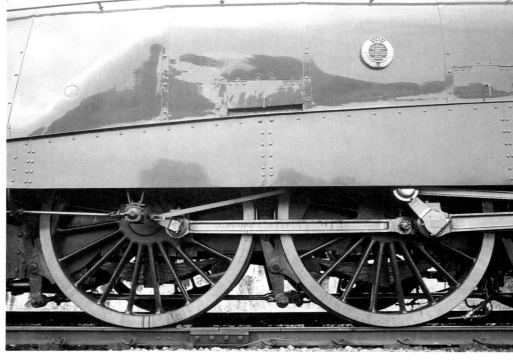

FAR LEFT: *The controls of the record-breaking* Mallard.

CENTRE, LEFT: Mallard's *fire-door.*

BOTTOM, LEFT: *The rear coupled wheels of* Mallard, *half-hidden by the streamlined valance.*

LEFT: *The commemorative plaque recording* Mallard's *world record.*

RIGHT: Mallard's *nameplate.*

BELOW: *After withdrawal from active service* Mallard *became a museum engine, but was then restored to working order in celebration of the 50th anniversary of its record-breaking run. Here it is seen hauling an excursion train through the Chilterns in 1986, soon after its restoration.*

"Mons Meg"

FRANK NEWBOULD

EDINBURGH
TRAVEL BY L·N·E·R EAST COAST ROUTE

LEFT: *Another LNER poster, advertising the attractions of Edinburgh.*

RIGHT: *An East Coast express in BR days hauled by the Gresley Pacific* Woolwinder. *The locomotive has been fitted with a double chimney, around which is an experimental smoke deflector. The coaches are in the standard British Railways maroon livery of the 1950s and 1960s.*

BELOW: *A modernistic representation of a Gresley Pacific in a poster of the 1930s.*

train that was identical with that of the 'Coronation' except that no observation car was provided. Like the other two luxury streamliners, it was orientated towards the businessman, running on weekdays only and with a schedule designed to suit those who had meetings in London. It left Bradford soon after 11am, and Leeds at 11.30am, and deposited its passengers in Kings Cross Station at 2.15pm, with the return northbound service leaving London at 7.15pm. Between London and Leeds the average speed was 68mph, but as the A4 Pacific did not work between Leeds and Bradford, a pair of 0-6-2 suburban tank engines were used instead. Two A4s, with names suggestive of the West Riding's main industry, were allocated to this train, *Golden Fleece* and *Golden Shuttle*. Like those allocated to the 'Coronation', they were painted blue with stainless-steel numbers and letters. Only one train set was needed for this service, but the LNER built five such trains for its luxury services, one each for the 'West Riding Limited' and 'Silver Jubilee', two for the 'Coronation', and one spare.

There was another LNER streamliner, the 'East Anglian'. This was an attempt, at the lowest possible expense, to provide the people of Norwich and Ipswich with a train that seemed the equal of the 'Silver Jubilee'. Two of the not especially fast 'Sandringham' class 4-6-0s were streamlined, renamed *City of London* and *East Anglian*, and provided with a new six-car train set which was open-plan and offered passengers meals at their seats. There was no supplementary fare and although the 57mph average between Ipswich and Norwich was high for that part of the country, it was low in comparison with the 'real' LNER streamliners.

Meanwhile the German railways had established a new maximum steam locomotive speed record of 125mph. While some LNER engineers regarded this as a challenge, there were others in management who were unhappy with the idea of running trains at speeds of that magnitude. But one of the consequences of previous high-speed running was anxiety about braking distances, and there were frequent Sunday brake-test runs on the LNER main line, in which high speeds were part of the work. In July 1938 one of these special trains was selected for an attempt on the record, although the Westinghouse Brake Company's specialists, travelling on the train, were unaware of this until the train had left its starting point, just north of Grantham. The A4 *Mallard* was at the head, and was driven hard, reaching 126mph near Essendine. This effort, which remains the world's record for steam traction, was not without its cost, because *Mallard's* middle big end, the Achilles Heel of Gresley's 3-cylinder designs, overheated and failed, although the locomotive was able to reach Peterborough before being retired to the engine shed.

On the LMS, there was no attempt to match the 'West Riding Limited' between London and Leeds, but in the Anglo-Scottish service the LMS 'Coronation Scot' did offer reasonable competition. The LMS suffered from the handicap that the West Coast Route was not suited for such high speeds as the East Coast Route. Not only did it have speed restrictions through such junctions as Rugby, Stafford, Crewe and Preston, but, in its northern section, trains had to climb to 915 feet above sea level at Shap, and 1015 feet at Beattock, the Shap and Beattock climbs being separated by the descent into Carlisle, practically at sea level. Moreover, loadings were quite heavy on the West Coast Route, thanks partly to the

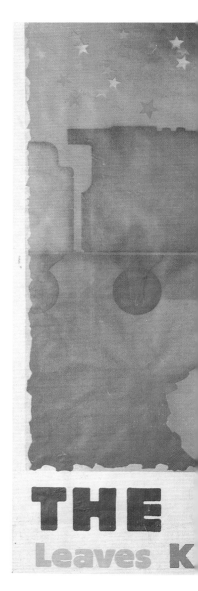

THE
Leaves K

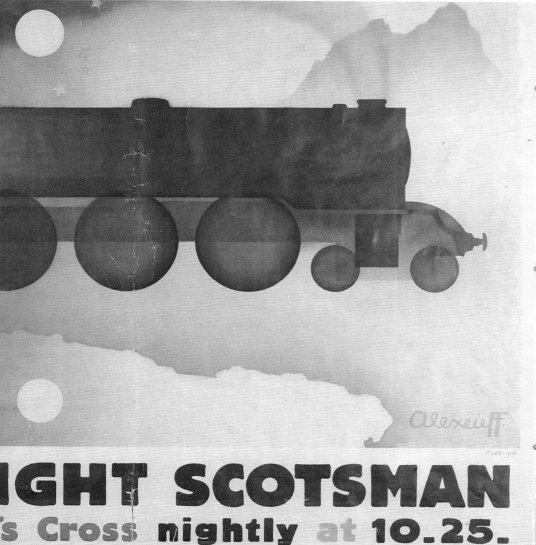

IGHT SCOTSMAN

's Cross nightly at 10.25.

traffic potential of Glasgow. The supplementary-fare 'Coronation Scot' was probably the best solution to these problems. It was quite heavy, it was fast, and it was, ostensibly, streamlined.

When it was introduced, the 'Coronation Scot' comprised nine coaches, weighing about 300 tons. They were of standard design, but the streamlined locomotive with its blue and white stripes that were continued down the sides of the coaches, gave an impression of a completely streamlined train. In 1939 some better rolling stock was built for the service. This was painted in LMS maroon with gold stripes, and some of the streamlined Pacifics were painted to match. These new cars, with a Pacific, were sent to the USA for exhibition at the New York World Fair. There they were overtaken by war, and although the locomotive was soon returned, the vehicles remained in the USA until the end of the War, by which time the 'Coronation Scot' had been discontinued.

The 'Coronation Scot', with its 1.30pm departures from Glasgow and London, was a replacement for the old 'Midday Scot'. The morning 'Royal Scot' continued to run, but received less of the limelight. In the difficult 1920s it had been a double-headed train, with a pair of ex-LNWR locomotives as far as Carnforth, and then a pair of Midland compound 4-4-0s onwards. When the 'Royal Scot' class 4-6-0 was introduced, this was one of the first trains entrusted to the new power, enabling double-heading to be eliminated. From 1932 progressive accelerations were made, and by 1939 it covered the 299 miles to Carlisle at an average of 60mph. For a train which could sometimes amount to 15 coaches, this was good running, made possible by the introduction of Stanier's Pacifics.

By that time the 'Royal Scot' had sections for Glasgow, Edinburgh, and Aberdeen. Unlike so many other named trains, it continued to run through World War II. It lost its restaurant cars and its Aberdeen section, but a second train, running five minutes behind the main train, ran to Perth and had through coaches to Thurso for the use of the Navy. At 721 miles, this London to Thurso service was Britain's longest through run and took just over 21 hours. After the War the 'Royal Scot' was very slowly restored to a semblance of its pre-war schedule of seven hours for the London-Glasgow run, but only in 1952, when it was equipped with new rolling stock, was an 8-hour timing achieved. Often 16 coaches were hauled, although during the War 17 had sometimes been taken.

The corresponding LNER train, the 'Flying Scotsman', was also accelerated in the 1930s. It usually ran in two sections, the first section was non-stop, and took seven hours for the London-Edinburgh run by 1937. In 1938 a new train set was introduced, with pressure ventilation and other luxuries, which increased the train weight so that with a 14-coach load, which was not uncommon, the train weighed 500 tons. At peaks, 15 or even 16 coaches were hauled, with through coaches for Edinburgh, Glasgow, Perth and Aberdeen. During the War the train continued to run as a London-Edinburgh

service without restaurant cars, and, in the early part of the War, it frequently comprised 20 coaches and once or twice went as high as 23, weighing about 800 tons gross. As early as October 1945, there was a partial return to the pre-war situation, with an 8-hour schedule and restoration of dining facilities. The Glasgow section began to run as a separate train and, by 1955, the London-Edinburgh schedule had been cut to seven hours.

But the 'Flying Scotsman' was no longer a non-stop service. Instead, the 'Capitals Limited' was introduced, preceding the 'Flying Scotsman' by half an hour and running non-stop to Edinburgh. It had a section for Aberdeen, which was thereby brought to 11 hours 50 minutes from London. In 1953 this train was renamed the 'Elizabethan', and the London-Edinburgh schedule reduced to 6¾ hours. A4 Pacifics were used, and, despite their age and less-than-perfect maintenance, usually succeeded in keeping this schedule with the normal eleven-coach train.

Dieselisation was soon followed by the disappearance of this named train, as of so many others in the Anglo-Scottish service. But the 'Royal Scot' and 'Flying Scotsman' names lived on into the age of diesel and electric traction, even though the titles became more a mark of tradition than a symbol of exclusivity.

ABOVE: *One of the LNER 'Green Arrow' 2-6-2 engines in 1959. These were small editions of the Gresley Pacific and often hauled the heavy East Coast expresses when a Pacific was not available.*

RIGHT: *In the 1950s British Railways introduced a number of new named trains, most of which were short-lived. A Scottish example was the 'Saint Mungo', here seen at Perth in the charge of a standard BR mixed-traffic 4-6-0. A Gresley Pacific is in the background.*

CROSS-COUNTRY AND COMMUTER TRAINS

LEFT: *A Southern Railway 4-4-0 with a south coast stopping train crossing the Brighton viaduct.*

CROSS-COUNTRY AND COMMUTER TRAINS

In some circles there was a regrettable tendency to regard any long-distance train that did not start and terminate at London as simply a 'cross-country' service. This was not the practice of the companies that operated such trains, usually at express speeds and with good-quality rolling stock. The term 'inter-city' was not used to describe a category of trains, but it would have been a more accurate description than 'cross-country' for services like those, for example between Edinburgh and Glasgow, where two companies fought the competitive battle with smart trains, tightly scheduled.

The true cross-country trains were an answer to the public's preference for through services, for changing trains was never popular. A network of long-distance services grew up, putting a very large number of cities and towns in direct communication with one another. Sometimes between two cities there might be only one daily through train, and it might not be very fast, but at least it enabled the passenger to settle comfortably in one seat for the whole journey.

One important cross-country flow was from the north to the southwest, and there were several companies competing for this traffic. Through trains were run, with the several companies providing locomotives for their section of the run and a proportion of the rolling stock needed. Such trains, quite often, consisted of two companies' coaches, each in their own livery, bringing, for example, the salmon-pink rolling stock of the LSWR to York, or the chocolate and cream of the GWR to Bradford.

The Midland Railway, and its successor the LMS, was well-placed to develop this traffic flow, with its line from Derby through Birmingham and Gloucester to Bristol and Bath. At Derby, it connected with its own main line from London to the north, and at Bristol, with the GWR. Moreover, with the LSWR, it shared ownership of the small but strategic Somerset & Dorset Railway, which ran trains over the Mendips from Bath down to Poole and Bournemouth. The MR ran a number of Bristol-Bradford and Bristol-York services, but also profited from holiday traffic to Bournemouth and the resorts served by the Great Western. In time, two of the better through trains were given titles to emphasise their function as holiday services. These were the 'Devonian' and the 'Pines Express'.

The 'Devonian' received its name in 1927, and was really only a Bradford-Bristol train carrying some through vehicles which were handed over to the GWR at Bristol for movement on to Torquay and Paignton. In the 1930s it offered a schedule of 8 hours 26 minutes over the 323 miles from Bradford to Paignton. This was not especially fast, but the average was lowered by the comparatively slow GWR segment of the trip, whereas it averaged 60mph over some sections of the LMS. The most testing trial for the locomotive was in the northbound direction, with the 2-mile drag out of Bristol at gradients varying from 1 in 90 to 1 in 70 and then the Lickey Incline at Bromsgrove, where a banking locomotive had to be used for the 2¾-mile 1 in 37 incline. When the 3-cylinder 'Jubilee' class locomotives became available, they were almost invariably provided for this train.

The predecessor of the 'Pines Express' was initiated by the LNWR in 1910, and provided a service from Manchester to Bath and Bournemouth over the LNWR, MR, and Somerset & Dorset. It received its name under LMS auspices in 1927. When it was restored after World War II, it provided a 7-hour transit from Manchester to

Varieties of British suburban tank locomotive

Railway and class	Year	Wheel arrangement	Cylinders (ins)	Coupled wheel diameter	Grate area (Sq ft)	Boiler pressure (psi)	Tractive effort (lbs)	Weight on coupled wheels (tons)
LSWR M7	1897	0-4-4	18×26	5ft 7in	20	175	19,750	35
GCR A5	1911	4-6-2	20×26	5ft 7in	21	180	23,750	54
GNR N2	1920	0-6-2	19×26	5ft 8in	19	170	19,950	57
LMS 4P	1927	2-6-4	17×26	5ft 3in	17	200	21,500	47
GWR 8100	1938	2-6-2	18×30	5ft 6in	20	225	28,200	53
LNER V3	1939	2-6-2	(3) 16×26	5ft 8in	22	200	25,000	57

LEFT: *Emett, the* Punch *cartoonist, makes his own comment about London commuters.*

ABOVE: Galatea, *of the LMS 'Jubilee' class, halts at Bromsgrove with the 'Devonian'. A banking locomotive (whose smoke can be seen at the back of the train) is being attached for the Lickey Incline.*

Bournemouth, in spite of the steep gradients on the S & D section. It was one of the few named trains to be frequently hauled by a 2-8-0 locomotive, the Midland Railway having built a batch of that type for the heavily-graded S & D.

A competing route from the north to the southwest was offered by the LNWR and GWR through Crewe, Shrewsbury, Hereford and the Severn Tunnel. The LNWR brought trains from the north into the joint station at Shrewsbury where a GWR engine replaced the LNWR locomotive. Then the train proceeded across the picturesque terrain of the Welsh Marshes and, at Newport, either turned west for Cardiff, or east for the Severn Tunnel, and thence to Bristol and Devon. This service became very popular and, by the 1940s, was presenting the GWR 'Castle' class engines stationed at Shrewsbury with some very hard tasks as they hauled the heavy loads over the undulating Marshes.

The GWR had other routes, too. Because it had the right ('running powers') to operate trains over parts of the Midland Railway south of Cheltenham, it could schedule trains from Birmingham over its North Warwicks Line to Stratford-on-Avon, Gloucester and thence to the southwest. On summer Saturdays, one train followed on the heels of another as Midlanders made their way to and from the Devon and Somerset holiday resorts. The route via Stratford-on-Avon also enabled the GWR to run a fast

Birmingham-Cardiff service in addition to its other Birmingham-Cardiff trains by the longer route through Worcester. These Birmingham-Cardiff trains, in the last days of the GWR and the early years of BR, were usually hauled by old 'Saint' class 4-6-0s of the Churchward era, which were still sprightly with the trains of six to eight coaches used on these services. The afternoon train to Cardiff from Birmingham, which, in the late 1940s, consisted of elderly coaches hauled by an even older engine, was the best of these trains, and ran the 120 miles in 2 hours 50 minutes with stops at Stratford, Cheltenham, Gloucester and Newport. This performance, given the difficult post-war situation, was regarded as very creditable.

One of the most interesting, and indeed unexpected developments of the north to southwest routes came with the expansion of the Great Central Railway, at the beginning of the century. Having engineered its 'London Extension', the GCR proceeded to lay a short line from its new route to connect with the GWR at Banbury. This line, inconspicuous on the railway map but laid to main-line standards, proved to be strategically very important, both to the GCR and to Britain in two world wars. Over it, in co-operation with the GWR, the GC soon began to operate cross-country freight and passenger trains. The passenger trains included expresses between Newcastle and Bournemouth, Manchester and Dover, Halifax and

LEFT: *The 4-4-0* Sir David Stewart *storms up to Kittybrewster with a summer excursion from Aberdeen in 1952. The Great North of Scotland Railway used similar 4-4-0 locomotives for all its trains, which served the small towns of north-east Scotland and barely earned their keep. When the GNSR became part of the LNER there was little change, and the 4-4-0s survived on their original, undemanding, duties into BR days.*

CROSS-COUNTRY AND COMMUTER TRAINS

Ilfracombe, Bradford and Bournemouth and Newcastle and Barry.

The last of these became the 'Ports to Ports Express', and was extended to Swansea. It was remarkable in that its route included the sleepy Cotswolds single-track GWR line through Bourton-on-the-Water between Banbury and Cheltenham. This line was too lightly laid to take the bigger locomotives, and even in its later years the GWR was providing one of its lightweight 'Manor' 4-6-0s for the service. With a usual load of six coaches, of which one was a restaurant car, the 45 miles from Banbury to Cheltenham took 82 minutes, although the train ran considerably faster than this on other sections. Overall, the Swansea-Newcastle trip took exactly ten hours.

Other cross-country runs were to be found throughout Britain. Indeed, lesser companies like the Cambrian or the Great North of Scotland railways might be described simply as operators of cross-country trains, since they had no dense inter-city routes. The GNSR, serving a thinly populated region of eastern Scotland, had only one real traffic centre, Aberdeen. It operated short trains hauled by small 4-4-0 locomotives and, with highway competition still in the future, just managed to make a living from what were, in effect, simply local trains. The Cambrian was in a similar situation, with Shrewsbury as

its largest traffic centre, but it did operate express trains over its singletrack line across central Wales.

An important cross-country service was one operated over the Pennines by the Lancashire & Yorkshire Railway. The best train, introduced in 1908, between Liverpool, Manchester and York, boasted a 12-wheel dining car for its first-class patrons as well as a more modest dining car for third-class passengers. The Lancashire & Yorkshire's massive 'Atlantic' locomotives were usually used on these trans-Pennine trains, including this one.

'Local' trains was an elastic term. On some railways, any train that was not an express was a local. On others, the description excluded suburban services. The typical local train, however, ran between adjacent centres, calling at all stations. It provided a local transport function, but for the railways was also important as a feeder and distributor of passengers for the long-distance trains. At a time when car ownership was small and bus services sparse, a large proportion of long-distance travellers started and finished the railway journey at a local station, rather than at a big city station. Local trains usually used old rolling stock handed down from express service, and the present-day preservation of many celebrated passenger locomotives, like those of the Midland

ABOVE: *A north to south holiday train of the 1950s: a former LBSCR Atlantic (a design derived from the Great Northern Atlantic) at Redhill with a Birkenhead to Brighton train.*

LEFT: *A Wainwright 4-4-0, demoted from mainline service, hauls a stopping train from Reading to Tonbridge in 1950.*

RIGHT: *Morning commuters embark at Ilford. One door for each compartment was characteristic of suburban coaches, avoiding the need for a corridor and helping to reduce loading times.*

Compound, Wainwright 4-4-0 and several others, was possible because these time-expired engines survived into the age of preservation, thanks to their usefulness as tractive power for local trains.

In terms of numbers of passengers carried, it was the suburban trains that made by far the biggest contribution to the statistics. In the last half of the nineteenth century, the railway companies had done their utmost to develop daily short-distance travel into and out of the cities. Cheap fares, in the form of workers' tickets and season tickets, were among the blandishments offered, as well as an intense service of trains, especially at the beginning and end of the working day. Socially, these services were an enormous gain, enabling people to live outside the often insalubrious cities where they worked. From the railways' point of view, however, the encouragement of suburban traffic was unfortunate. Trains provided for the traffic peaks lay idle most of the day. The passengers were short-distance and travelling at reduced fares, while costs per passenger were quite high.

Managements, and especially designers of locomotives and rolling stock, therefore sought trains that would handle the greatest number of passengers for the smallest cost. Using elderly mainline coaches for suburban work was never very practical, because the comfort and facility requirements of long-distance passengers represented simply a waste of space for short-distance travel. When suburban traffic developed, in the

UPPER LEFT: *During World War II, first-class vehicles were removed from many suburban trains. Here a train indicator at Waterloo Station in London marks such trains with special discs.*

LEFT: *Another World War II London scene: passengers patiently await news of their train at Liverpool St Station.*

ABOVE: *A 2-4-2 tank locomotive of a type built in large numbers by the London & North Western Railway for suburban service. Many of them survived into the 1950s, including this example, which was photographed at Warwick with a two-coach stopping train from Coventry.*

culated principle, with each pair of permanently coupled coaches sharing a common bogie in the centre. Running in eight-car sets, having twelve bogies instead of the conventional sixteen, these trains could seat 632 passengers for a tare weight of only 147 tons.

The other extreme was represented by the heavy vehicles, built by the Great Central for its outer suburban services from Marylebone Station. Running non-stop through the inner suburbs to the leafy residential areas of the Chilterns, they provided almost mainline comforts, with four-a-side seating in first class and five-a-side in third, with both classes having reading lamps attached to the partitions.

In the inter-war period, the four wheelers finally disappeared, together with some of the older bogie coaches. The replacement stock was all-steel, with increased comfort in the third class at least. However, the fundamentals of suburban coach design still had to be observed, including such items as fast-opening and closing doors for each compartment to reduce station times, maximum number of seats per ton of vehicle, implying six-a-side in third class and the absence of toilets and corridors. It was not until the era of the diesel train that a few of these standard specifications were eventually changed.

For handling suburban trains, tank locomotives were obviously advantageous; they were able to run comfortably in either direction, and at each terminus could be shifted to the other end of the train for the return trip without having to go to a turntable first. The suburban tank locomotive became a definite locomotive category, beginning with 2-4-0 types in the nineteenth century, and ending with the big 2-6-4 types, built by British Railways. Of the 2-4-0 variety, the GWR 'Metro' tanks were perhaps the best known, but none has been preserved. The LSWR 2-4-0 tank engines, of which one has been preserved, were interesting in that they carried most of their water not in side tanks but lower down, between the frames.

From the 2-4-0 developed the 2-4-2, the extra pair of carrying wheels providing a smoother ride when moving bunker-first, as well as enabling more coal to be carried. This, in turn, enabled engines to make longer runs before going to the locomotive depot for coaling, and the demand for this type reflected the spread of the suburbs outwards, with better-off passengers living many miles out of town. The Lancashire & Yorkshire, Great Eastern, and London & North Western railways were great users of the 2-4-2 tank engine, with many examples of the type surviving long enough to be used by British Railways.

At this point of suburban locomotive development, progress began to take different directions. On the one hand there was a demand for locomotives that could handle the outer-suburban services. These tended to have longer distances between stops, which favoured locomotives with a higher speed capacity. On the other hand there was simply a requirement for bigger engines that could handle heavier trains at the same speeds on the inner suburban services. To provide faster locomotives meant somewhat larger driving wheels, although the difference was not great, because the outer-suburban trains did stop quite frequently and large driving wheels, admirable for speed, would have worsened the accelerative capabilities that were equally important for reducing the overall journey time. Speed also demanded a smoother running locomotive, with carrying wheels

last quarter of the nineteenth century, it was customary to provide special rolling stock, typically, high-capacity, close-coupled, four-wheel coaches, marshalled into trains of about fifteen vehicles. There was little luxury, except in first class, and the decor was usually austere. Third-class coaches were often compartmented only by low partitions, making them open-plan in appearance, if not in practice. Third-class seating was five-a-side, on wooden benches, while second class provided the same space, but had the addition of seat cushions. First class, however, provided more space, with passengers sitting four abreast and with only four compartments per coach.

Six-a-side seating, bringing a sizeable cost benefit but imposing a perceptible degree of discomfort on passengers, especially when winter clothing was in season, appeared in the years before World War I. The GER was among the earliest to introduce this unwelcome improvement, and was so pleased with the result that it took its existing suburban four-wheelers, cut them longitudinally down their centres, and spliced in an extra width of roof, floor, and seating to produce six-a-side stock. On the Great Northern Railway, which operated a busy suburban service out of Kings Cross Station, with small tank locomotives facing quite stiff gradients, increasing the number of passenger seats per ton of train was especially important. Nigel Gresley, soon to be locomotive superintendent, but at the time carriage and wagon superintendent, built some unique suburban trains on the arti-

both fore and aft. From the 2-4-2, therefore, evolved the 2-6-2 tank locomotive, which tended to have driving wheels of around 5ft 6in. The 4-4-2 also became quite popular, and was often simply a tank engine version of a railway's 4-4-0 mainline passenger engine. In the 1930s, the LMS, followed in the 1940s by the LNER, favoured the 2-6-4 tank locomotive for outer-suburban services. This was because the trailing bogie was able to carry more coal and water.

For slower suburban trains, the provision of carrying wheels to provide a smoother run in either forward or reverse motion was less important. On some railways, including the MR, LSWR, North Eastern and Caledonian railways, the 0-4-4 tank locomotive became very popular. This was a medium size locomotive with a very generous coal capacity. However, it was a rough-rider except on the very best track or at the most moderate speeds. Rough-riding was also a characteristic of the 0-6-2 tank locomotive. This wheel arrangement was favoured by, among others, the Great Northern, Great Central, and Great Eastern railways as well as the LNWR. The small railways of South Wales also liked it, probably because more of the engine weight was concentrated on the driving wheels, the extra adhesion being valuable for haulage up the mining valleys. Later, the GWR built itself two hundred of the type for use in South Wales. In general, locomotives designed for the shorter suburban runs had

driving wheels of around 5ft diameter, giving them good acceleration and, in the case of South Wales, making them equally suitable for freight haulage.

In the early twentieth century, a handful of companies built very large suburban tank locomotives for particular traffic. The Great Central, for example, built a series of 4-6-2 tank locomotives for heavy suburban trains, while the LBSCR built a pair of very handsome 4-6-2 tank engines, *Bessborough* and *Abergavenny*, for its best businessmen's Brighton-London service. This pair lasted into BR days, although some LBSCR 4-6-4 tank engines did not survive long in their original form. On the whole, the LBSCR, with its dense suburban network, preferred the 4-4-2 wheel arrangement, and produced an outstandingly efficient design. But due to the rapid electrification of suburban lines south of London by the Southern Railway, the LBSCR as well as the SECR and LSWR, suburban tank locomotives did not last long on the work for which they were designed.

It may not be accurate to describe the 50-mile London-Brighton run as a suburban service, although the later term, commuter service, would be quite correct. In general, the better-off salaried class was prepared to travel an hour or more from its city jobs, so Brighton-London was in spirit, if not by definition, a suburban service. The Cambridge-London service, provided by the GNR and its successor the LNER, advertised as the

ABOVE: *A Leamington to Birmingham suburban train near the end of its journey in the 1950s. These GWR trains, hauled by 2-6-2 tank locomotives like this one, were formed of four-vehicle sets which in the peak hours were coupled together to form eight-coach trains.*

RIGHT: *On the former London Tilbury & Southend Railway, here shown in LMS days, the suburban service was so dense that locomotives carried destination boards to help passengers and railway staff.*

LEFT: *A local train comes off the Tay Bridge at Dundee in 1956. The coaches are of LNER pattern while the tank locomotive is one of a 2-6-4 taper-boiler series introduced by Stanier of the LMS for outer suburban services.*

BELOW: *The original LMS 2-6-4 tank engine had a parallel boiler and was designed by former Midland Railway engineers. This example shows one hauling a Shrewsbury to Swansea train.*

'Cambridge Buffet Expresses', but known to undergraduates as the 'beer trains', would hardly qualify, as although they took little more than an hour their infrequency did not attract the season-ticket holder.

On the other hand, the Blackpool 'Club Train' of the Lancashire & Yorkshire Railway was certainly a commuter service, even though it resembled an exclusive express. This train enabled salaried workers to live in the Blackpool area while working in Manchester, and in the early twentieth century it comprised eight coaches, of which three were first class and two 'club'. The club coaches were strictly members-only vehicles. Members were first-class season-ticket holders, elected by the 'carriage-committee'. Having been duly elevated to this privileged situation, they were required to pay the quite hefty membership fee and obey the club rules, which included such provisions as a ban on open windows while the train was in motion. Apart from exclusiveness, the only advantage of membership was the service of a carriage attendant, who provided tea *en route*. The LNWR introduced similar club trains between Manchester and Llandudno. The NER, while not providing a club train, was also trying to persuade the better-off to travel further to work when it introduced fast trains for season-ticket holders between Bradford and Scarborough. These were summer-only services, the assumption being that the families of well-to-do breadwinners would settle in the seaside resorts just for the season.

However, these long-distance commuter services were exceptional. More typical were the intensive medium- and short-distance services operated out of London and the big cities. In these, the proportion of short-distance services tended to diminish as electric tramways took over much of the business. But pressures were hardly eased by this, for medium-distance passengers not only increased in number but also in expectations. Hammering the railway managements had

TOP: *One of the capable 4-4-2 tank locomotives of the LBSCR. Built for London commuter services, these engines were soon displaced by electrification; this example was photographed in the 1950s with a country train near Tunbridge Wells.*

ABOVE: *A South Wales suburban train. The 0-6-2 tank locomotive formerly belonged to a Welsh company, the Taff Vale Railway, but was rebuilt, GWR-style, after the Taff Vale became part of the Great Western.*

become a favourite preoccupation of the popular press, and suburban services, inevitably overcrowded and congested in the peak periods, were a sitting target.

The SECR, in its final years, did succeed in creating order out of previous chaos. This Railway had two busy London commuter termini at Charing Cross and Cannon Street, with another big station at London Bridge. A great user of 0-4-4 tank engines, the SECR typically operated 13-car suburban train sets weighing only about 138 tons while carrying about 30 tons of passengers. Despite their 500-passenger capacity, there were simply not enough of these trains to cope with growing traffic, and line congestion precluded a more intensive peak-hour operation. But by restructuring a few key junctions, revising the timetable so as to avoid conflicting train movements at junctions, making use of all possible re-

serves at the termini (that is, utilising mainline engines to remove empty trains, specifying the exact positions of locomotives awaiting their next duties, assembling trains that were as long as the platforms could accommodate, and a host of lesser measures), the SECR found it had extra train capacity, and with this margin introduced bigger and more punctual service. Nevertheless, with steam traction and conventional mechanical signalling, paths could be provided for 30 trains per hour into Cannon Street.

Steam traction, in the form of 2-4-2 and 0-6-0 tanks, was also performing well on the Great Eastern Railway our of Liverpool St Station in London, pulling trains of fifteen 4-wheel coaches. On the eve of World War I, more than 100,000 passengers were making a daily return trip into this terminus, making it the busiest for suburban traffic in the country. It was noteworthy for other features, apart from intensity. From 1897, it offered a half-hourly all-night service on its Walthamstow line. Its twopenny return workmen's ticket for the 21-mile Enfield-London line was said to offer one of the world's best miles-per-penny bargains.

At the beginning of the century, this service also brought into being one of the most remarkable locomotives ever built in Britain. In an attempt to cream off the GER's more intense traffic flows, a new electric railway was promoted from London into the eastern suburbs. With electric traction, claimed the promoters, schedules would be shorter and more accommodation could be offered. To refute this claim, the GER locomotive superintendent, James Holden, was instructed to build a viable steam locomotive capable of equalling the accelerative powers of an electric train. That is, the 30 seconds needed by the current 0-6-0 tank locomotives to accelerate the 240-ton trains to 20mph was to be improved on, so that a 300-ton train would reach 30mph in 30 seconds from a standing start. Holden dutifully produced the most powerful steam locomotive yet seen on a British railway. It was of the 0-10-0 wheel arrangement, another first for Britain, and was a tank locomotive with three cylinders and a massive wide firebox. On trial, it bettered the GER directors' requirements, and its performance, widely reported, helped to defeat the parliamentary bill of the electric railway promoters. Having thereby fulfilled its purpose, the 'Decapod' was soon converted into a more useful engine, as it was too heavy to use regularly on the GER suburban lines.

After World War I, traffic out of Liverpool St continued to increase, to a point where severe congestion was experienced, as reduced office hours meant that the peaks were concentrated into a shorter time-span. Capital was not available for electrification, so a careful study was made and a radical plan put into practice. Tracks were rearranged to avoid conflicting movements, and each suburban platform was given its own engine dock, where locomotives from incoming trains could go without interfering with trains on other tracks. A few extra signals and crossovers were installed along the lines, and 16-coach trains were standardised for the peak hours. These provided 848 seats, which meant that there were now enough seats for all passengers. To speed movement, the exits from all platforms could be used by passengers arriving at any platform, and first-class coaches had a yellow stripe, and second-class a blue stripe, painted between the windows and roof. This latter idea was the origin of the 'Rainbow Service' nickname bestowed on these trains.

ABOVE: *Cross-country electrification as presented by* Punch.

Trains arriving at Liverpool St Station unloaded their passengers, deposited their engine in the engine dock, attached a locomotive at the outer end, and were away from the platform within four minutes, freeing it for a following train. At the peak, 24 trains left Liverpool St in the hour, a rate of 340 seats per minute. On some routes, capacity had been increased by 50 per cent by these improvements, and it probably represented the maximum attainable with steam traction and mechanical signalling.

In the inter-war years, while electrification overtook most of the London suburban lines south of the Thames, steam continued to provide a good service elsewhere. The GWR had sizeable suburban operations not only out of London, but also from Birmingham and Cardiff. The latter were modelled after those of the previous smaller railways absorbed by the GWR, and notably after those of the Taff Vale Railway, whose 0-6-2 tank locomotives remained in service for several decades. The GWR replaced old suburban coaches with all-steel trains, marshalled as 4-coach sets, which, in peak hours, were joined to form eight-car trains.

For its London and Birmingham services, the GWR relied on its several series of 2-6-2 tank locomotives with 5ft 8in driving wheels, and derived from a design dating from the Churchward years. Several of these have been preserved, as indeed have other suburban tank designs. This high survival rate is partly due to the large number of suburban locomotives that were built, but mainly to the usefulness of the type for preserved railways. The same features required for suburban services have proved equally useful for tourist line operation.

LEFT: *On the former Great Eastern suburban service out of Liverpool St Station. The coaches are LNER, but the engine is still of GER design even in the 1950s when this photograph was taken.*

ABOVE: *An 0-4-4 suburban tank locomotive of the South Eastern & Chatham Railway, now preserved.*

RIGHT: *One of the 0-6-2 tank locomotives used by the GNR, and later the LNER and BR, for suburban services out of London. This engine, designed by Gresley, is now preserved in working order.*

HEAVY FREIGHT AND FAST FREIGHT

LEFT: *A West Coast freight train climbing to Shap in the final year, 1967, of British steam. The locomotive is a 'Britannia' Pacific.*

HEAVY FREIGHT AND FAST FREIGHT

Of the four big railway companies formed in 1922 only one, the Southern Railway, made more money from passengers than from freight. Freight haulage, though less interesting to outside observers, was the mainstay of most railways even though the first inter-city line, the Liverpool & Manchester, had been built primarily for passengers.

By the twentieth century, British railway freight operations were already very different from those in other countries. This was largely because archaic techniques had been retained. Foremost among these were the loose chain-and-hook couplings, employed for freight wagons, and the absence of a centrally controlled train brake. Trains were assembled by shunters, armed with hooked poles with which they coupled or uncoupled the chains. Train speed was controlled by the locomotive brakes, aided by the guard in his heavy brakevan at the rear, which had its own set of brakes. At the top of severe gradients the train would be stopped and the lever-operated wagon handbrakes would be pinned down to provide additional brakepower.

From 0-6-0 to 2-10-0: some salient freight locomotive designs

Railway	Year	Wheel arrangement	Cylinders (ins)	Coupled wheel diameter	Grate area (Sq ft)	Boiler pressure (psi)	Tractive effort (lbs)	Weight on coupled wheels (tons)
LSWR	1897	0-6-0	19×26	5ft 1in	20	180	23,500	47
GWR	1903	2-8-0	18×30	4ft 8in	27	225	35,400	67
MR	1911	0-6-0	20×26	5ft 3in	21	175	24,500	49
GCR	1911	2-8-0	21×26	4ft 8in	26	180	31,300	66
LNWR	1912	0-8-0	20×24	4ft 5in	24	175	28,000	62
LMS	1935	2-8-0	18×28	4ft 8in	29	225	32,400	62
BR	1954	2-10-0	20×28	5ft 0in	40	250	39,700	77

Driving a freight train required far more skill than handling a passenger train. On an undulating line parts of the train could be climbing, and other parts descending, and the ideal of having the wagons either gently pushing against each others' buffers or having their coupling chains fully extended under moderate tension was hard to achieve, even when the driver and the guard were experienced and alert. Sudden snatches of the couplings sometimes could break the train, and on a sharp curve they might even derail it. Wagon axle bearings were very simple and often ran hot, risking a fire if the train was not stopped in time and the defective wagon set out. The substitution towards the end of the century of grease lubrication by oil only partially alleviated this problem. Slow speeds were necessarily the rule, although this was not considered important for most bulk freight, even

though it resulted in abysmal labour productivity. In the nineteenth century, freight which required a fast transit was sent by passenger train, which is why mail, newspapers, parcels, and some other consignments, became part of the passenger business.

In the late nineteenth century freight requiring fast transit grew, and the railways began to operate fast freight trains. These could not rely on loose couplings and handbrakes, so an increasing proportion of freight wagons was equipped with the continuous automatic brake and screw couplings hitherto confined to passenger stock. Freight trains were classified according to the proportion of braked vehicles that they contained, these being marshalled next to the engine so as to be under the control of the driver. As the brakes were expensive and added weight, a number of wagons were fitted simply

ABOVE LEFT: *Milk churns being handled at one of the London stations in 1894. Even before the introduction of milk tank cars, Londoners benefitted from a growing rail movement of milk.*

Evolution of the mixed traffic locomotive

Railway	Year	Wheel arrangement	Cylinders (ins)	Coupled wheel diameter	Grate area (Sq ft)	Boiler pressure (psi)	Tractive effort (lbs)	Weight on coupled wheels (tons)
4300	1911	2-6-0	18×30	5ft 8in	21	200	25,700	53
H15	1914	4-6-0	21×28	6ft 0in	30	180	26,200	58
N	1917	2-6-0	19×28	5ft 6in	25	200	26,000	52
K3	1924	2-6-0	18×26	5ft 8in	28	180	30,000	61
Hall	1928	4-6-0	18×30	6ft 0in	27	225	27,300	57
'5'	1934	4-6-0	18×28	6ft 0in	29	225	25,500	53
V2	1936	2-6-2	(3) 18×26	6ft 2in	41	220	33,700	66

with the air pipe that operated the brakes. Such 'piped' rolling stock could be marshalled between the 'fully-fitted' vehicles without interrupting the continuity of the brake line.

Slow-moving bulk freight, however, predominated. Coal was by far the most important load. Some London rubbish was already being sent out of town by the train-load, and so was horse manure, collected at large stables and consigned to agricultural users. China clay was sent regularly from Cornwall to the Potteries, potatoes seemed to be sent in all directions, while ores were despatched to manufacturing areas and in due course were put back onto the railways in the form of ingots, semi-finished products, and manufactured goods. In the days before the motor truck appeared, whatever was marketed depended on rail at some stage in its production.

Every railway handled coal, frequently in block trains. It was the dominant fuel for industry, for homes, and for the railways themselves. Several small railways in South Wales were absolutely dependent on coal traffic, and the prosperous North Eastern Railway was almost in that position too. In South Wales the coal was brought down the valleys in short trains hauled by tank engines. When it reached Cardiff, it was sent to the railway-owned docks for export or bunkering, or assembled into coal trains destined for England through the Severn Tunnel. Much of it, loaded in distinctive wagons labelled LOCO, was sent by the trainload to the GWR locomotive depots. Until the coal industry was nationalised, each coal company had its own wagons, painted in distinctive colours, so coal trains were multi-coloured even if the predominant colour was black. By providing its own wagons, the coal industry saved the railways a good deal of capital investment, although this was balanced by the

ABOVE: *A GWR freight yard in the early twentieth century.*

RIGHT, ABOVE: *One of thousands of privately-owned, wooden-bodied, hand-braked, coal wagons circulating on the British railways up to the late 1940s.*

RIGHT: *The Devonshire apple crop is loaded at Newton Abbot in 1908.*

LEFT: *One of the powerful 2800 class 2-8-0 heavy freight locomotives built by the GWR from 1903 up to World War II. This was one of the later batches, with a more comfortable side-window cab.*

BELOW: *Some collieries had their own railways and locomotives, and the Lambton Colliery even had its own 'main line'. This 0-6-2 tank engine once hauled coal trains for its owner, the Lambton Colliery.*

RIGHT: *An 0-6-0 of the North Eastern Railway, one of the biggest coal-hauling railways.*

defective maintenance which these wagons often endured, frequently showing itself in breakdowns in transit. Moreover, the coal-owners were reluctant to change to larger capacity wagons. Their vehicles, typically of only 10 tons capacity, were inefficient compared to the 20-tonners that most railways would have preferred.

The GWR developed several locomotive types with the South Wales coal traffic in view. Most notable of these was the mineral 2-8-0 of the 2800 class, whose combination of pulling power and mechanical simplicity made it probably the best mineral engine ever used in Britain. The GWR also produced a 2-8-0 tank locomotive, rather unusual for Britain, for handling the short-distance coal trains, as well as some 0-6-2 tank engines for work up the Cardiff Valleys. For the mainline coal trains it had relied on 0-6-0 engines in the early years, then built a moderately successful class of 2-6-0s before making its somewhat expensive but worthwhile investment in 2-8-0s.

Other railways were less progressive than the GWR. The North Eastern Railway, which also had a big coal traffic originating in its territory and destined for export as well as home consumption, simply enlarged the 0-6-0 when heavier trains were needed. Its 0-8-0s, with their entire weight placed on the coupled wheels, could certainly pull, but like the 0-6-0s were rough-riding and unkind to the track at speeds above 20mph. Other big users of the 0-8-0 were the London & North Western and the Lancashire & Yorkshire railways. The L & Y 0-8-0s could haul 2300 tons on level track, although in practice their trains were smaller than that. The LNWR and L & Y lines had to wait until the 1930s before they received the new LMS-built 2-8-0 locomotives.

The Great Central Railway, which served the south Yorkshire coalfield, was also a user of the 2-8-0, and its design was destined to be adopted by the government as a war-service locomotive in World War I. After that war, some units were sold by the government to the British railway companies and the GWR was among those which bought a batch. The attraction of the GCR 2-8-0 was its resistance to misuse, as it was a simple locomotive solidly built. It also had a very good boiler which, according to its most passionate admirers, could raise steam with just a candle in the firebox.

In Scotland, both the North British and the Caledonian railways originated a good deal of coal traffic, but relied for the most part on 0-6-0 types to handle it. But the biggest, and least justifiable, use of the 0-6-0 was to be witnessed on the Midland Railway, later LMS, main line from the Nottinghamshire coalfield to London.

Why the Midland Railway insisted on using engines too small for the traffic offered, remains a mystery, although it has been suggested that the in-breeding of managerial and engineering staff in its headquarters town of Derby was so deep as to make it almost impossible to introduce radical new thinking. The MR had used 0-6-0s to haul its freight in its early days, and 0-6-0s were still used 80 years later. However, by the 1920s the trains were much heavier, so it had become the practice to use two engines per train, a highly uneconomical procedure. In 1925, when the MR had become the LMS but the situation on its lines hardly changed, 70 freight trains a day were leaving Wellingborough for the south, of which 50 were coal trains and almost all of those coal trains were double-headed. Under LMS auspices, 33 Garratt patent locomotives were ordered from Beyer-Peacock for these Midland coal trains. The Garratt locomotive, virtually two engines in one, certainly eliminated much of the doubleheading but, because the LMS locomotive department at the time was under strong Midland influence, the manufacturers were obliged to incorporate MR practice in the design, so these Garratts were hardly the last word in locomotive technology.

The Great Northern Railway was also fighting hard for its share of the Nottinghamshire coal traffic, and it, too, relied on the 0-6-0. However, early in the century it

invested in some 0-8-0s, which it used for coal trains from Nottingham to London and also for some of the very heavy Fletton brick trains. But in its last year of independent existence the GN introduced the more sophisticated 2-8-0 wheel arrangement in engines designed by Nigel Gresley.

Mineral traffic engines used driving wheels of less than 5ft diameter. The smaller wheel produced more tractive effort while its unsuitability for high speed was irrelevant for the haulage of trains that were always regarded as low-speed drags. The favourite wheel diameter for British mineral locomotives was 4ft 8in, and, of the 'Big Four' post-amalgamation companies, only the Southern Railway was without such locomotives. This Railway, having little freight traffic, had no specifically heavy freight locomotives apart from a handful of tank engines, so all its freight trains were hauled by mixed-traffic locomotives.

The LMS at last began to receive modern mineral traffic locomotives in the 1930s, with the introduction of William Stanier's Class 8F 2-8-0, of which nearly 700 units were eventually built. This was a very successful design, Stanier having learned much during his days in the GWR mechanical engineering department. It was chosen as a standard war-service type in World War II, and was built in the workshops of the other companies as well as of the LMS. Some units were sent to the Middle East, where they remained at work into the the 1980s.

In addition to the Stanier 8F, the British government also purchased a new type of 2-8-0 specially designed for war conditions and known as the 'Austerity' 2-8-0. The dimensions were almost identical with the 8F, but differed greatly in appearance, having been designed for economy of materials, ease of maintenance, and speed of construction. Many units were sent abroad, but, after the War, large numbers were purchased by British Railways. One batch of these capable, if unappealing, locomotives was built to the 2-10-0 wheel arrangement, and apart from the solitary Lickey Banker

LEFT, TOP: *One of the Beyer-Garratt locomotives bought by the LMS for coal traffic. Despite their deficiencies, these locomotives did eliminate doubleheading on the trains from the East Midlands coalfield.*

ABOVE: *The 'Jones Goods', the first 4-6-0 in Britain, introduced by the Highland Railway in 1894 for its freight trains.*

LEFT: *A Stanier '8F' heavy freight locomotive of the LMS. This engine has been preserved.*

treated as passenger trains by the operating authorities. They were regular, they were timetabled, and their progress was telegraphed in advance down the line.

With town populations increasingly dependent on food brought in from the ports or from agricultural areas hundreds of miles distant, a large number of fast freights had to be run for perishables. At the end of the century, the LNWR's 'Scotch Fish and Meat' was probably the best of these. It left Carlisle just before 9pm and arrived at the Broad Street goods station in London about 5am. Its speed was such that it was sandwiched throughout its run between two overnight express passenger trains, running ten minutes behind the 'Limited' and half an hour in front of the 'Special Mail'. This train supplied the London markets, and its meat and fish were on sale in the shops the morning after their despatch from Scotland.

Some railways operated regular fish trains, among them the North British, serving the Aberdeen fishery and handling also the fish vans originating in the small ports, served by the Great North of Scotland Railway. But it was the Great Central which, serving Grimsby, could be regarded as the premier line for fish. It actually built 4-6-0 locomotives with the fish trains' requirements as part of the specification, and it operated these trains not only to London but to Manchester and also to places on the GWR via Banbury. The Grimsby-Manchester fish train across the Pennines did the difficult trip in just over six hours. The unpredictability of daily fish arrivals meant that these trains could vary in size from day to day. The Grimsby-Manchester fish train on some days did in fact exceed the 45-van maximum permitted load, and this demanded great skill from the locomotive crew. GCR 4-6-0s continued to haul these trains up to the 1930s, but in due course the new LNER K3 type 2-6-0s took over.

The fish travelled in unrefrigerated vans, but were packed in ice inside boxes. The dripping of the melted ice was a characteristic of these trains as they proceeded on their way. The smell was also a distinguishing feature, but they were not the smelliest of trains. The manure trains, which gradually ceased to run as large concentrations of horses died out, probably held that distinction, but block cattle trains were also easily distinguishable in the dark.

Quite strict regulations controlled the carriage of livestock. Horse transport was part of the passenger business, but other livestock went by freight train. Since cows had to be watered once a day, and milked as well, it was in the railways' interest to run cattle trains as fast as possible, and such trains fell into the category of fast freight. Sheep were a little easier to handle, as they only needed to be watered every 36 hours, but they, too, had the benefit of movement by the faster trains.

In the inter-war years, with government subsidies to aid dairy farmers, the long-distance carriage of milk from distant areas to the cities created a demand for specialised milk trains, which usually ran at night, so that the evening's milking could be on city doorsteps the following morning. From the early days of railways, milk had been habitually carried, usually on passenger trains in churns, with farmers delivering their churns to local stations for movement to the nearest town. But by the 1930s, whole trains of glass-lined tank wagons, owned by dairy companies, were sent from dairying areas like Devon and Cornwall into London. Some of these trains included flat-cars on which rode rubber-tyred tank trailers, which completed their trip to the London dairies by road. This was an early example of 'piggyback' transport.

0-10-0 and the GER's 'Decapod', these were the first locomotives with ten coupled wheels to operate in Britain. Among the range of standard designs initiated by BR was a new class of 2-10-0 with 5ft wheels, the Class 9F. Intended for heavy freight, this type was so well-balanced that it could operate at the higher speeds, being quite suitable for fast freights and also, when necessary, passenger services.

Although the fast freight train was a late nineteenth-century creation, the railways had certainly realised at an early stage that some freights needed to be faster than others. Low-value bulk commodities like coal, ores and timber could tolerate slow transits, but manufactured goods and consumer supplies needed something faster. By the end of the nineteenth century, shippers were demanding, and usually getting, trains that enabled them to hand over their consignments in the early evening for delivery in another city the next morning. Fast freights were therefore, typically, night freights. This suited the railways, because at night there were very few passenger trains occupying the lines. It suited clients in many ways, depending on their business, but this was an age in which speed of transactions was becoming commercially important. The whole tone of the British industrial economy depended on the ability, for example, of a Yorkshire businessman to travel to London one morning, attend a sale of Australian wool, place his order, return home, go to bed, and find the consignment of wool already at his mill the next day.

Although there were no mixed-traffic locomotives designed as such, the railways could usually find suitable locomotives for fast freights from among their passenger locomotives. Some railways, notably the LNWR, Caledonian, NER, and GCR, built 4-6-0s especially for fast freights. As the rolling stock provided for these trains was selected from the vehicles with continuous brakes, ordinary freight locomotives, which were not equipped with such brakes, could not have been used even if they had been fast enough. The really fast freights were in fact

The Great Western Railway was deeply involved in the long-distance milk business, as well as in other perishable traffic, which, more often than not, was seasonal. It ran trains of ventilated vans for Cornish broccoli, for example, and also handled cut flowers from the Scilly Isles. From Weymouth, in season, it despatched Channel Islands new potatoes. Also, for a few weeks each year its Cheddar Valley branch despatched strawberries by the vanload.

Among fruits, bananas required the most careful handling and punctuality. Several railway companies were involved with the operation of 'banana specials', which ran as a matter of urgency when banana boats arrived in port. As the transport of this fruit was calculated as part of the ripening process, schedules had to be carefully maintained, while special banana vans were used to guarantee correct packing and ventilation. The GWR from Avonmouth, the SR from Southampton, and the LMS from Liverpool were the main participants in this traffic.

The unspecialised, or mixed, express goods train developed rapidly after World War I, when highway transport began to cream off high-value traffic from the railways. Manufactured goods, sent by the vanload rather than the trainload, were ideal targets for the new breed of road hauliers, who could offer a door-to-door service which was faster than the railways over short and medium distances. The railways did not want to lose this traffic, because it was charged at high rates, and therefore responded with an improved service of general merchandise trains.

Such trains had existed in the pre-war years. Indeed, as early as the 1840s, the LNWR was despatching ten regular general freights northwards out of London each day. They were not fast, but to places like Birmingham and Manchester they could offer an overnight service. Birmingham, for example, was less than seven hours from London by freight train even at that early period. But with the advent of properly braked rolling stock much better performances became possible. By World War I, the Great Northern Railway was taking

great pride in its express freights which, composed entirely of braked rolling stock, averaged 40-45mph. The Great Eastern introduced its first fully-braked train in 1906, and by 1914 was operating four of them. They ran between Spitalfields, in London, up to Doncaster and averaged 40mph for much of the trip. They were limited to 25 vehicles, plus a brakevan for the guard, and were hauled by 4-4-0 locomotives of the 'Claud Hamilton' type, which were among the GER's best express locomotives. As the GER used the Westinghouse air brake for its passenger services and the freight vehicles used the vacuum brake, these locomotives had to be fitted with both kinds of brake. Later, it was found possible to adapt the air brake to suit both vacuum- and air-braked trains.

TOP, LEFT: *A milk tank car which once brought Somerset milk to London overnight, returning empty in the day.*

TOP, CENTRE: *A GWR fruit van, designed with special ventilation and internal fittings to make it suitable for Worcestershire plums and apples.*

ABOVE, LEFT: *A milk train of the GWR, hauled by No.4700, one of a small class of fast 2-8-0 locomotives.*

TOP, RIGHT: *A pre-war exhibition, one of several organised by the LNER to advertise its freight services at a time of stiff competition from road transport. Centre of attention here is the newly-built* Green Arrow, *the 2-6-2 designed by Gresley with fast freight trains in mind.*

ABOVE: *The Midland Railway preferred small engines, but built this large 2-8-0 as one of a class of locomotives intended not for itself but for its jointly-owned Somerset & Dorset Joint Railway. Crossing the Mendips south of Bath, this line had stiff gradients, and these locomotives were often used on passenger as well as freight trains.*

By the 1940s, the GER's four daily express freights had expanded, under LNER auspices, to several times that number. This was partly due to the need to match road competition, partly to the rise of small industries in Great Eastern territory. Some of the new trains were named, for example the 'Lea Valley Enterprise' served a new industrial area while the 'Essex Express' served the Chelmsford area. That other component of the LNER, the former GNR lines, also maintained the tradition of fast freights. In the 1930s, from late afternoon until late evening, a succession of such trains left London with a return flow also commencing in those hours. Naturally enough, the longest-distance trains started first, with the 'Three-Forty Scotsman' leaving London for Scotland just before the 'Three Fifty-Five Southerner' left Glasgow on the return working. There were several cross-country fast freights in the LNER timetable as well, with Liverpool-Newcastle and Hull-Nottingham forming two of the main arteries.

The advent of purpose-built, mixed-traffic locomotives assisted the development of the fast freight network. It is true that the 0-6-0 had for decades been regarded as a maid-of-all work, and it continued to be used in several roles almost up to the end of the steam era with, for example, the LMS continuing to build and use Midland Railway designs not only for freight, but also for local trains and excursions, while on the LNER Gresley's more modern J39 0-6-0 showed similar versatility. However, the real mixed-traffic locomotive could tackle fast expresses at one end of the range and heavy freights at the other, so it was not the fastest of passenger engines nor was it suitable for handling the very heaviest freights, but it could cope with everything in between, and with fast freights it was at its optimum.

The GWR 2-6-0 of the 4300 class that appeared in 1911 is regarded as the first of this new category of locomotive. With coupled wheels of 5ft 8in diameter, midway between the 6ft 8½in of GWR express engines and the 4ft 7½in of the heavy freight engines, it was ideal both for the average passenger train and the average goods train, but excelled with fast freights. Several hundred were

LEFT: Green Arrow, *after several decades hauling passenger and fast freight trains, was withdrawn for preservation and later restored for active operation. This picture shows it with a Manchester to York excursion.*

TOP, RIGHT: *Another view of* Green Arrow.

ABOVE: *One of the light 4-6-0 locomotives built by BR, with a stone ballast train. Much railway freight was hauled for the railways' own benefit; locomotive coal and track ballast were especially heavy traffics.*

FOR PARTICULARS OF

FACTORY SITES

OR VACANT PREMISES ON
THE L·N·E·R SYSTEM IN
ENGLAND OR SCOTLAND APPLY TO

THE INDUSTRIAL AGENT

KING'S CROSS STATION   LONDON N1

TELEPHONE TERMINUS 4200   EXTENSION 3396

built, but the GWR soon moved on to larger mixed-traffic types. The 4700 class was an enlargement of the 2-6-0, being a 2-8-0 with a large boiler and 5ft 8in coupled wheels. Consisting of only nine locomotives, this class was used on the GWR's night freights, and was rarely seen in daylight hours, except when it was pressed into summer passenger train service. The inter-war 'Grange' and 'Manor' 4-6-0s were also enlarged 2-6-0s and the former, in particular, proved to be a very capable machine, while the smaller 'Manors' enabled lightly-laid lines to enjoy the services of modern 4-6-0 locomotives. The most numerous GWR mixed-traffic design, the 'Hall' type, was derived not from the 2-6-0, but from the 'Saint' express 4-6-0. In fact, the prototype 'Hall' was simply a 'Saint' rebuilt with 6ft instead of 6ft 8½in coupled wheels.

The larger wheel diameter, compared with other mixed-traffic types, made the 'Hall' slightly better for fast passenger work and not quite so good for heavy freight, and the GWR was not alone in building two kinds of mixed-traffic locomotive with differing sizes of coupled wheels.

On the LMS Railway, there was a similar sequence. First, in 1924, came the ugly but effective 'Crab' 2-6-0, with a wide boiler, 5ft 6in coupled wheels, and designed in the L & Y Railway tradition because the LMS chief mechanical engineer at that time was a former L & Y man. When Stanier joined the LMS in the 1930s, he designed an equivalent of the 'Hall' 4-6-0, the celebrated Class 5, of which over 800 units were built. Their dimensions were almost identical, but in some roles they performed slightly better thanks to a larger superheater.

LEFT: *A publicity photograph which shows great care in producing a headboard, but little attempt to clean the locomotive; it therefore dates, probably, from the late 1940s.*

RIGHT: *A Southern Railway 4-6-2 tank locomotive, one of a small class designed to transfer freight vehicles between London freightyards. It is shown leaving Feltham Yard.*

BELOW: *The LNER mixed-traffic 4-6-0, introduced during World War II as the B1 class.*

The LNER, when it was formed, already had the K2 2-6-0 designed by Gresley for the Great Northern, and from 1924 built the same designer's K3, which had a bigger boiler, three cylinders, and the same 5ft 8in coupled wheels. The K3 was an immediate success, especially on fast freights but, twelve years later, was partly superseded by the celebrated V2, a 2-6-2 with 6ft 2in coupled wheels. The V2 became a successful passenger engine, and, during World War II, hauled unprecedentedly heavy express trains, but it was introduced largely with the LNER's fast freights in view. The first unit was named *Green Arrow*, that being the brandname of a fast freight service then being advertised by the LNER. The final LNER mixed-traffic engine was a 4-6-0, the B1 type, which also had 6ft 2in coupled wheels and, like the V2, was used more often on passenger trains than on freights.

The Southern Railway used two types of 4-6-0, the S15 and H15 classes, for some of its freight trains. These were LSWR designs and differed mainly in the diameter of their coupled wheels, which were respectively 5ft 7in and 6ft. The SR did not possess any heavy mainline freight locomotives, so its goods trains were hauled either by these 4-6-0s or by smaller types. The latter included various 0-6-0s but, more importantly, the various 2-6-0 types which the SR inherited from the South Eastern & Chatham or built on the basis of SECR designs. The SR also inherited the very handsome Class K 2-6-0s from the LBSCR which remained in service for many decades, having made their debut on World War I munitions trains to Newhaven docks.

After nationalisation, British Railways built more mixed-traffic engines, including a new version of the LMS Class 5 with 6ft 2in coupled wheels. Rather unexpectedly, the heavy freight Class 9F 2-10-0 proved to be an excellent mixed-traffic design, too.

The biggest and the smallest.

LEFT: *A diminutive 0-6-0 tank engine built by the South Eastern & Chatham Railway shunts freight vehicles at Brighton in 1951.*

BELOW: *The enormous, by British standards, Garratt locomotive introduced by the LNER for pusher service in the Pennines. It had eight driving axles, and remained a sole example. The photograph shows it on trial as a banker for the Lickey Incline, far from its original territory.*

Apart from the extension of fast freight services, inter-war freight operations were also characterised by developments in wagons, which tended to be more varied in design and function and also, on average, slightly larger. In the early twentieth century, most railways had a preponderance of open cars. About 60 per cent of the LNWR's 60,000-strong freighter stock, for example, was accounted for by such vehicles. Many of these had a central bar on which a tarpaulin could be spread, and much traffic, which might have been expected to move in vans, was hauled under tarpaulins. The LNWR possessed only about 5000 vans. By 1914, the biggest wagon-owner was the Midland Railway, with about 119,000 units, of which 12,400 were vans, 18,300 mineral wagons, and 82,300 non-mineral open wagons. The NER occupied second place with 118,000, but 60,000 of those were mineral wagons, reflecting the North Eastern's main preoccupation.

In the inter-war period new, more specialised wagons were built. The tank car for oil products and chemicals became commonplace. More vans and fewer tarpaulined open cars were used. The demountable road/rail container was introduced to enable the railways to offer door-to-door service. Other specialised vehicles included new designs of insulated vans for meat and other perishables, and the LNER had a brick wagon capable of carrying 20,000 bricks.

Attempts to introduce larger wagons were only partly successful. The coal companies, reluctant to reconstruct their loading facilities, resisted the introduction of bigger coal wagons, so wagons of ten tons capacity, or even less, continued to be used. The GWR, and some other railways, built 20-ton coal wagons for their locomotive coal, and the NER, before it was amalgamated into the LNER, introduced an all-steel bogie coal wagon of 40 tons capacity. In the 1930s the GWR built long-wheelbase vans of 20 tons capacity, and the other three railways made similar advances. But, in general, wagons remained small, and wooden-built stock predominated. The British railways had begun the century with a technical lag as far as freight rolling stock was concerned, and by the time of nationalisation were still lagging behind other countries.

ABOVE: *An LMS Class '5' locomotive. Hundreds of this very useful mixed-traffic 4-6-0 were built. The example shown is one of the later batches, with a modified front end. The 'SC' on the smokebox door denotes a self-cleaning smokebox (that is, the soot was blown out of the chimney rather than heaping up inside the smokebox, an innovation that was not everywhere regarded as an improvement).*

RIGHT: *A 'County' class 4-6-0 of the GWR gets away from Swansea with a parcels train.*

ON THE BRANCHES

LEFT: *Branchline trains at Torquay in 1922. The locomotives are of the 4500 class of light 2-6-2 tank, used by the GWR for many of its West-Country branches.*

Before the wholesale line closures of the 1960s, British railway branch lines were so numerous as to be an integrated and expected part of the landscape, a British institution. And yet, although the peculiar and intimate branchline atmosphere was so familiar and omnipresent, the lines were all very different and it is hard to categorise them. The typical branch line was from two to twenty miles long, singletrack, and operated by small and elderly locomotives,. But the Swansea branch of the LNWR was 115 miles long, the Kingswear branch of the GWR carried express trains hauled by 'King' class locomotives, and several branches were doubletrack. In Ireland, there were long branches built to the broad gauge (that is, to the Irish standard gauge of 5ft 3in) as well as a host of other highly individual 3ft gauge lines.

The old companies built branch lines with an enthusiasm that their successors would later regret, for such lines were hard to operate at a profit in the age of the country lorry and country bus. Yet when they were built, these lines enabled local communities to break out of their commercial and social isolation. Not only could they get the daily London newspapers on the day of publication, but also perishables like Lyons cakes and day-old chicks. Trips to the market town became suddenly easier and therefore more frequent. Local producers, especially farmers, found that they could market a wider range of products further afield. Many branch stations were provided with extensive goods yards, for freight traffic could be very important, and in later years many branch lines lost their passenger trains while remaining open for freight.

The GWR, and occasionally the LMS, built engines specifically for branchline use, but the common practice was to use old locomotives, typically suburban tank engines that had become too small for their original duties and 0-6-0 tender engines which, likewise, had become outclassed for freight work on the main line. To simplify operations. various types of push-pull trains were put into service. These proceeded normally in one direction, but simply reversed for the other direction,

Purpose-built branchline locomotives

Railway and class	Year	Wheel arrangement	Cylinders (ins)	Coupled wheel diameter	Grate area (Sq ft)	Boiler pressure (psi)	Tractive effort (lbs)	Axle-weight (tons)
GWR 4500	1906	2-6-2	17×24	4ft 7in	17	200	21,250	15
GWR 4800	1932	0-4-2	16×24	5ft 2in	13	165	14,000	14
BR 2	1953	2-6-2	16×24	5ft 0in	17	200	18,500	13
BR 2	1953	2-6-0	16×24	5ft 0in	17	200	18,500	13

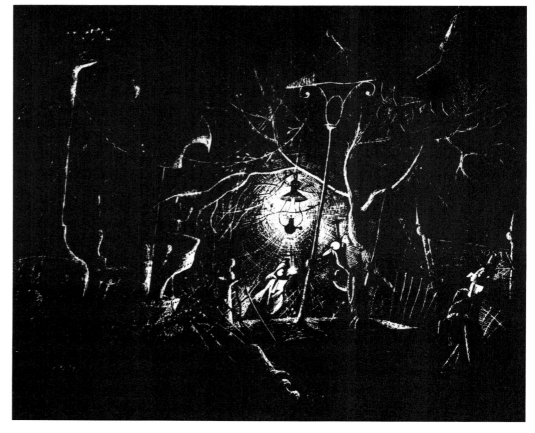

ABOVE: *A few British branch lines were independent, never becoming part of the major companies or of BR. Behind the fantasy of this* Punch *cartoon lies an exaggerated but not untruthful impression of these eccentric lines.*

LEFT: *A former Caledonian Railway 0-4-4 tank locomotive of a type frequently used on Scottish branches.*

RIGHT, TOP: *A typical GWR branchline junction. This is Yatton, junction for the Clevedon branch.*

RIGHT: *One of a small batch of 0-4-4 tank locomotives built by the LMS specifically for branchline service.*

the locomotive driver transferring to a special cab installed at the end of the outer coach. He could leave the fireman on the engine and, through a system of wires which varied between the different companies, would drive the engine by remote control.

A predecessor of these trains was the steam railmotor, in which the passenger coach at one end rested on a normal bogie, but at the other end was permanently attached to a diminutive 0-4-0 steam locomotive. These units, which were in essence steam-powered rail buses, promised substantial cost reductions on branches where passenger traffic was light and where a turnaround loop was not provided at the outer end. Some had vertical boilers, but most used a conventional horizontal boiler, where the engine part of the vehicle rather resembled a small shunting locomotive. On the LNWR and GWR, however, the engine was enclosed with the coach body, for aesthetic reasons, with only the driving wheels and the extreme top of the chimney revealing the existence of the engine. Some of the rail motors supplied to the Taff Vale Railway and LBSCR were not 0-4-0 but 2-2-0 in wheel arrangement.

The rail motors worked reasonably well, and could pull a trailer car, but, when traffic increased to a point where more than two vehicles were needed at peaks, a conventional train had to be used, with the rail motor lying out of use. Because of this inflexibility of the rail motors, the companies increasingly turned to the push-pull operation with small tank engines, which were sometimes sandwiched in the middle of the train. Many of the rail motor bodies were converted to driving trailers for these push-pull trains. The GWR variety, which survived in large numbers until the 1960s, was bow-ended, uncompartmented, with longitudinal seats along the sides and had a large slatted floor area. This was to provide a safe standing space, as well as a suitable place to dump the often rough and heavy baggage brought along by passengers of these trains on market days.

The GWR was unusual in having built new tank engines for these trains in the 1930s. The original locomotives had been 2-4-0 Metro and 0-4-2 tank engines, displaced from city suburban services, and the new engines, built to replace them, were 0-4-2 tanks of almost identical design, except that they had all-over cabs. The GWR also built some 0-6-0 tank engines for branches requiring extra tractive power.

Of the four inter-war railways, only the GWR had any semblance of standardisation in its branch trains. For the shorter branches a push-pull set, called auto-train on the GWR, was used. Usually the motive power was one of the modern 0-4-2 tank engines, but sometimes an 0-6-0 tank was used and, in very rare cases, old nineteenth century suburban tanks were still in use. Such branches frequently connected a country town to the main line, and had no intermediate stations. The Clevedon branch was typical of these, but there were many more, including those to Wallingford, Cirencester, Oswestry, Abingdon, and Marlborough. These branch trains would spend much of their time waiting at the junction for mainline connections, and the service was sometimes surprisingly frequent. For example, on weekdays 26 trains left Yatton for the return trip to Clevedon.

Yatton was also the junction for one of the GWR's longer branches, through Cheddar to Witham. This was a 31-mile line, although most of the trains turned round halfway, at Wells. The GWR had introduced locomotives for this kind of branch line, too. Beginning with a small

LEFT: *A former GWR auto-train coach forms the rear of a train on the present-day Torbay steam railway.*

LEFT, BELOW: *A GWR auto-train at Llantrisant in the 1940s. It has just arrived, locomotive pushing at the rear, from Pontypridd, over the line of the former Taff Vale Railway. The locomotive is a 2-4-0 tank engine which in its youth, a half-century previously, had worked in the London suburban service. A GWR milepost is at the left.*

RIGHT, TOP: *The wide sweep of the bay at St Ives. This poster shows the view offered to passengers arriving by the branch train.*

BELOW: *A GWR 4500 class 2-6-2 tank engine restored for working on the Torbay steam railway in Devon. The driving end of an auto-train coach can be seen next to the engine. This railway, which is a restored GWR branch using former GWR locomotives, runs from Paignton to Kingswear.*

batch of 2-6-2 tank locomotives with 4ft 1in coupled wheels, and which later found employment on the bleak and hilly Princetown branch. From 1906 the GWR built 2-6-2 tanks with 4ft 7½in coupled wheels, the 4500 class. These were sometimes used on suburban services, especially around Bristol, but were also a favourite type for the longer branches where, typically, they also tackled branch freight trains.

The 4500 class was widely used on the Cornwall branches, including the St Ives branch. This four-mile line, which left the London-Penzance main line at St Erth, was opened in 1877 and immediately transformed the fishing village of St Ives into a sought-after tourist resort. GWR publicity helped in this, especially in the inter-war years, and the sweep of the railway around the bay, alongside which it had its terminus, was a well-publicised attraction. Part of the 'Cornish Riviera Limited' was detached at St Erth, to proceed to St Ives behind one, sometimes two, of the 4500 class tank engines. The GWR's own Tregenna Castle Hotel helped to maintain the flow of first-class passengers and, on summer Saturdays, ten-coach trains were sometimes operated over the branch.

The GWR also had several branches operated by tender engines. The winding, picturesque line that dropped south from the Cambrian main line at Moat Lane to pass through the market towns of Llanidloes and Builth down to Brecon, was for long a preserve of the 'Dean Goods' 0-6-0, used for both freight and the widely-spaced passenger trains. Some of these were market-day-only services and others would only run on school

days. But the ubiquitous GWR 2-6-0 was the commonest engine for most of the longer lines, which included the Gloucester-Ledbury and the Taunton-Barnstaple branches.

The Barnstaple branch was rather exceptional, since although the majority of trains were three-coach (two non-corridors and one corridor), a few of them, especially in summer, were expresses from London and the Midlands which at Barnstaple were handed over to the Southern Railway for haulage to the seaside resort of Ilfracombe. To speed trains over this singletrack branch, the tokens that drivers carried over each block section as tangible proof of their right of way were not exchanged at signalboxes by hand, but picked up on the run from line-side token-exchange equipment, the locomotives being fitted with a pick-up on their cabsides. This line was also unique in operating rabbit specials for much of the year, with each local station loading consignments brought in by the local farmers and trappers.

Although the GWR branches presented quite a variety of locomotives and coaches, this variety was surpassed on the branches of the other three companies, which, for the most part, used old equipment handed down from their constituent companies. On the Southern Railway, for example, branches in Kent tended to use 0-4-4 tank locomotives that had once been in suburban service on the SECR, while, in ex-LBSCR territory, LBSCR tank engines were used. In the west, on lines formerly belonging to the LSWR, elderly 0-4-4 tank engines were the usual motive power, with old 4-4-0 and 0-6-0 tender engines on the longer lines.

ABOVE: *The two-coach GWR Carmarthen to Aberystwyth train sets out across the River Teifi in 1951. The locomotive is an 0-6-0 of a type introduced in the 1930s to replace the ageing 'Dean Goods' engines. The class was essentially of the same design as the older engines, but carried a tapered boiler and more comfortable cab.*

ABOVE: *A GWR 'Dean Goods' still at work in the mid-1950s on the Brecon to Moat Lane line, a singletrack low-traffic route joining southern and central Wales. The train is shown leaving Brecon, and consists of only two coaches. The lightweight rail can be seen; it was this weak track which enabled the 'Dean Goods', with their low axle-weight, to monopolise this line.*

RIGHT: *An M7 0-4-4 tank locomotive of the former LSWR. These engines, originally built for city suburban lines, were often used by the Southern Railway for branchline work.*

ABOVE LEFT:*A Padstow branch train leaves Wadebridge in 1955. The leading locomotive is one of the standard Southern Railway 2-6-0 type while the second is an old Drummond 4-4-0 of the former LSWR. The large eight-wheel tender of the latter was a common feature of locomotives originally built for the LSWR's mainline expresses, because absence of water troughs required higher water capacity.*

LEFT: *The three-coach Padstow section of a London-bound train leaves Wadebridge behind an SR 2-6-0 in 1955. In the foreground is one of the old LSWR 2-4-0 tank locomotives used for the Wenford Bridge branch line.*

ABOVE RIGHT: *The Exmouth branch train about to leave Exeter Central in 1949, headed by a former LSWR M7 type 0-4-4 tank locomotive.*

The SR's westernmost extremity was Padstow, reached by a branch from Wadebridge, which was itself connected by branches to Bodmin and Launceston. The 5-mile Wadebridge-Padstow line was operated as a continuation of the 7-mile Wadebridge-Bodmin branch, but by no means all the trains ran the full twelve miles. Most trains were short, hauled by an 02 class 0-4-4 tank locomotive, but longer trains, like the Padstow section of the 'Atlantic Coast Express', could have an ex-LSWR T9 4-4-0, or one of the newer 2-6-0s or, in the final years, a 'West Country' 4-6-2. At the same time, the GWR had running rights to Wadebridge from Bodmin Road on its London-Penzance main line. Bodmin was one of those small towns enjoying the luxury of service by two branch lines, the GWR line from Bodmin Road, and the SR branch from Wadebridge, with both providing connections to London. At Bodmin, both companies had a terminus, but the GWR, by reversing its train at Bodmin, could take its 4500 class 2-6-2 tank and two coaches right through to Wadebridge. Not far from Wadebridge, a freight-only line, kept open solely for china clay traffic, went to Wenford Bridge and provided employment for one of the earliest of the LSWR suburban tanks, whose 2-4-0 wheel arrangement made it the most suitable type for this sharply curving line. Another old LSWR suburban locomotive class, the 0415 4-4-2 tank locomotive of the 1880s, survived for similar reasons to work the Axminster branch in South Devon.

Other interesting SR branches in the southwest included the Callington branch, so steeply graded that it sometimes needed a pair of 02 tank locomotives to haul its passenger trains. Located not far from Plymouth, it had the advantage of providing a rare crossing over the lower Tamar and was therefore well-used. Then there was the narrow-gauge Lynton & Barnstaple, a picturesque line whose closure in 1935 aroused much opposition. Not far away, the SR was operating a branch that

had been built as late as 1925. This was the 20-mile Halwill-Torrington branch, which three times a day, in each direction, offered a usually empty train to the usually non-existent passengers. This was not the only new branch operated by the SR, for in Kent the company opened its Allhallows branch in the 1930s. This was intended to tap a new commuter area created by residential development, but the expected traffic never materialised. In the 1950s, an 0-4-4 tank of the former SECR was still hauling, eleven times a day, a train consisting of two former LBSCR coaches between Allhallows and Gravesend. The same locomotive class was also entrusted to another of the SR's more interesting Kent branches, the Elham Valley line. This had been built in the days when the South Eastern and the London Chatham & Dover railways were in cut-throat competition, and, to forestall the LCDR's attempt to reach Folkestone, the SER built this line from Folkestone to Canterbury. It was very picturesque but, like so many other branches, had too few passengers to survive, and the Southern closed it in 1947.

Another Southern branch, with origins in inter-company struggles, was the Meon Valley line. This was built by the LSWR to mainline standards to create an alternative route to Portsmouth, thereby forestalling the GWR's attempt to reach that area. Eventually, this line saw a handful of daily trains, hauled by one of the larger ex-LSWR M7 class 0-4-4 tank locomotives, but traffic was never more than sparse and the line was closed in 1955. But another line, not far away and also worked by M7s, lasted until 1973. This was the 'Watercress Line', so called because most of southern England's watercress was grown around one of its principal stations, Alresford. It ran from Winchester to Alton, and in its last years was served by former LSWR 2-coach push-pull trains. Part of it is now a steam-operated tourist line where locomotives much larger than the M7 can be seen at work.

On the lines formerly belonging to the LBSCR, the Southern Railway operated the branch lines, usually, with ex-LBSCR rolling stock. LBSCR 0-6-2 and 4-4-2 tank engines were often used, although the branch from Havant to Hayling Island was unique in using the tiny 'Terrier' class. These 0-6-0 tank engines, introduced for London suburban trains of the 1870s, were used on this branch because a rickety viaduct prevented the operation of anything heavier.

The LMS, biggest of the four companies, had the greatest variety of branch lines. These were worked by dozens of different locomotive types, reflecting the range of engines received from the old constituent companies. It was only in its final years that the LMS decided to replace this variegated stock, to which end it introduced, in 1946, a pair of new designs. One was a neat little 2-6-2 tank numbered in the 1200 series with 5ft coupled wheels, and the other, numbered in the 6400 series, was a tender version of this engine, with the 2-6-0 wheel arrangement but identical in all its main components. Construction of these types, slightly modified, was later continued by British Railways with the 84000 series tank and the corresponding 78000 series 2-6-0.

One of the first LMS branches to receive the new 1200 series locomotives, was the Coventry-Warwick-Leamington line, whose push-pull trains had hitherto been entrusted to elderly 2-4-2 tank engines that had once been the LNWR's main suburban locomotive type. These 2-4-2 engines, with slightly larger 0-6-2 tank engines, were the most common motive power for former LNW branches.

An exceptional branch was the Shrewsbury-Swansea line of the LNWR. This made use of much trackage

ABOVE: *A 2-6-0 locomotive type built by the LMS for branchline use and subsequently copied by British Railways. No.46444 is shown leaving Cambridge for St Ives in 1956.*

LEFT: *The Thurso branch train in 1951, in charge of* Ben Alder, *a former Highland Railway mainline 4-4-0. The picture was taken at Georgemas, the junction for the Thurso branch and the train is awaiting a connecting service from Inverness.*

RIGHT, TOP: *A former Great Eastern Railway 2-4-0 working on an East Anglian branch line in the 1950s. This locomotive was later preserved.*

RIGHT: *A push-pull train, propelled by a former SECR 0-4-4 tank locomotive, prepares to leave Goudhurst.*

OVERLEAF: *On the Keighley and Worth Valley Railway in 1986. The leading locomotive is an LMS 2-6-2 tank locomotive of the 1200 series, a small machine built in the 1940s for branchline service and later copied by British Railways.*

LEFT, TOP: *A Scottish branch train in 1956. A former North British Railway 0-6-0 takes the St Andrews train through Guardbridge.*

LEFT: *The Highland Railway's Dornoch Branch in 1951. An HR 0-4-4 tank locomotive approaches the mainline junction at The Mound.*

ABOVE: *A Great Eastern Railway 2-4-2 tank locomotive, originally built for London suburban service, still at work in 1951 with the St Combs branch train in north-eastern Scotland. The cowcatcher was fitted because this branch line, unusually for Britain, was unfenced.*

jointly owned by the GWR and LNWR and also of GWR track over which the LNWR had running powers. The route gave the LNWR access to Carmarthen and Llanelli as well, and the company was bold enough to offer a through London-Swansea passenger service via Shrewsbury, which was probably the most circuitous routing of any long-distance train in Britain at the time. In its early days, this line was operated by LNWR 0-6-0s, often doubleheaded because of the stiff grades. But shortly before World War I, the LNWR built some heavy 4-6-2 passenger tank locomotives, and some of these were allocated to the line. Later, under LMS ownership, the new 2-6-4 passenger tank locomotives were used, with ex-LNWR 0-8-0s for freight trains.

The LNWR also had a series of branch lines penetrating the northern ends of the South Wales coalmining valleys. On the map, these were quite isolated from the main LNWR system, but the Railway had running powers over a number of connecting lines. These other LNWR South Wales lines were also heavily graded. The 'coal tank', a 0-6-2 design with wheels small enough for freight operations, was used on these lines for passenger service, and towards the end of its independent existence the LNWR built some 0-8-2 and 0-8-4 tank locomotives for handling the coal trains of these lines.

On the former Midland Railway branches the motive power was usually an ex-MR 0-4-4 tank engine, with MR 0-6-0s being used for the longer runs and for freight. In the 1940s and 1950s, modern 2-6-2 tank loco-

motives replaced the 0-4-4s, and 2-6-0s began to replace the 0-6-0s.

Some of the most fascinating LMS branches were inherited from its Scottish constituent companies, the Highland and Caledonian railways. Britain's northernmost branch was that from Georgemas Junction to Thurso, a line that proved vital in World War I because of its sea connection with Scapa Flow. Between the wars, it languished but never died, and still exists today under diesel traction. In its last steam years, it was served by an old Highland Railway 'Ben' class 4-4-0. Another Highland Railway branch was from The Mound to Dornoch, one of those highly picturesque lines which never had much chance of making a profit. It was built as late as 1902 as a 'light railway', which under British legislation absolved it from the need to provide various safety measures, like manned level crossings, in return for a speed limit of 25mph. The HR's biggest branch, however, was to the West coast of Scotland at the Kyle of Lochalsh, a 63-mile line from the junction with its 'main line' at Dingwall. This was a mountainous route, and the 'Clan Goods' 4-6-0 was for long its mainstay.

Other long lines to the west coast of Scotland included the Caledonian Railway's Oban branch, which became part of the LMS, and the celebrated West Highland Railway of the North British Railway, which was absorbed by the LNER. The latter line, ending on the coast at Mallaig, 163 miles from Glasgow, was regarded as the most spectacular of all British railways. In the last

LEFT: *A former Great Eastern 0-6-0, now preserved in working order, hauls a tourist train near Sheringham in north Norfolk.*

ABOVE: *The Horncastle branch train performs its reversing act at Woodhall Junction in Lincolnshire. The engine is one of the Great Central 4-6-2 tank engines once used for heavy London outer-suburban traffic.*

RIGHT: *A former GNR 0-6-0 tank locomotive at work on the North Yorkshire Moors tourist railway.*

years of steam traction it was served by ex-North British 4-4-0s of the 'Glen' class, sometimes used in pairs, and by more modern 2-6-0s provided by the LNER.

The LNER branches in Scotland included many long lines formerly operated by the Great North of Scotland Railway. The terminus of one of these, the Ballater branch, was exceptionally well endowed because it was the railhead for Queen Victoria's favourite retreat at Balmoral. Another GNSR branch was from Fraserburgh to St Combs. This was unique in Britain because its locomotive was required to carry a cowcatcher, as the line was not fenced. In its later LNER days, the branch train was handled by a 2-4-2 tank, which had once hauled suburban trains out of London for the Great Eastern Railway.

The LNER, more than other companies, made a practice of allocating locomotives that it had acquired from one of its constituent companies to lines previously operated by other companies, so the sight of an ex-GER locomotive handling the traffic on a former GNSR branch was not all that exceptional. In Lincolnshire, where the LNER had inherited a network of branches from the Great Northern, GN 4-4-0s, 0-6-0s and 4-4-2 tank locomotives predominated, but the LNER did not hesitate to draft big ex-Great Central 4-6-2 tank engines for its Horncastle branch. A peculiarity of the Lincolnshire branch was that its junction with the main line faced the wrong way. The locomotive would propel its train backwards from the mainline station of Woodhall Junction, proceed for a few train-lengths to pass the points, and then set off forwards down the branch – a manoeuvre familiar to old-timers. It was thus quite in keeping with the British branchline tradition, with its comforting blend of the time-honoured and the unexpected.

STEAM TRAINS PRESERVED

LEFT: Leander, *a preserved 'Jubilee' 4-6-0 of the LMS, hauling an excursion train through the Welsh Marches in 1984.*

RIGHT: *No.2005, a preserved LNER 2-6-0 frequently employed on steam excursions in Scotland.*

OVERLEAF: *The preserved LMS Pacific* Duchess of Hamilton *hauling an excursion on the Settle & Carlisle line.*

The preservation of steam locomotives and old rolling stock has been carried much further in Britain than in any other country. The reasons for this lie in chronology, good luck, and the prevalence in Britain of a strong tradition of voluntary, sometimes eccentric, initiative. Chronology was important insofar as the end of steam came after the public consciousness had grasped that the preservation of past technologies was a worthwhile end. Geography played a part, because railway preservation schemes in a country like Britain were never too far from the population centres that would both provide the manpower and later the paying visitors. The big element of luck was that many steam locomotives sent for scrap at Barry in South Wales were not dismembered immediately, and the proprietor of this scrapyard was sympathetic to requests from locomotive preservation societies to keep specific locomotives intact until money had been raised to buy them from him. As for the voluntary spirit, few preservation schemes lacked members who were willing to devote weekend after weekend to the most laborious tasks, or who would find the necessary money out of their own pockets.

Typically, a locomotive would be 'rescued' by a group of individuals who established a locomotive preservation society for the purpose. They would first collect the money to purchase the locomotive from Barry at scrap prices. They would then need to negotiate hospitality from one of the preserved railways. This was usually easy, as it was a case of enthusiasts talking to enthusiasts. Then road transport of the locomotive had to be arranged, because after years in the scrapyard it was not fit for movement on rails. Then the locomotive would languish, after receiving a coat of paint to stop the rust progressing further, until labour and spare parts could be organised. Those societies which were early in their pilgrimage to Barry were more lucky than latecomers, because they were usually allowed to take away spare parts from other engines of the same design. But raising the money and finding volunteer workers was often a long drawn-out process.

For example, the BR 2-6-0 No. 76017, which began work on the Mid-Hants Railway in 1984, was the beneficiary of the society that called itself the Standard Mogul Preservation Group. This society was formed as early as 1972, raised the cash by 1973, and, after carrying out urgent maintenance at Barry, had the locomotive moved to the Quainton Railway Centre in Buckingham in early 1974. Some components, including a tender, had also been removed from Barry, from sister engine No. 76077. At Quainton some of the heavy preparatory work was done, like paint-stripping, and the boiler was given the required hydrostatic test. After this, from several possibilities, the society chose to remove its engine for further restoration and eventual operation to the Mid-Hants Railway. Complete restoration took several more years so that, in all, 12 years elapsed between the decision to save the engine and its entry into service. Other locomotives of the scores saved from Barry had similar histories. Some took much longer. The Mid-Hants Railways was one of several preserved lines which depended absolutely on locomotives from Barry.

Although some railways, like the GWR, are better represented than others, like the LNER, and although some locomotive types, like the LMS Class 5 and the GWR 0-6-0 tank engine, might be over-represented, in general a remarkably good cross-section of locomotives has been preserved. Most, naturally, are from classes that were still active in the 1960s, but, thanks to previous efforts by public-spirited individuals and organisations, quite a few of the earlier nineteenth century locomotives have also been saved.

In general, locomotive and rolling stock preservation can be divided into three modes. First there are the static railway museums, then there are the working

museums, in which locomotives actually work and move, and, finally, there are the steam excursions over BR main lines. The division between these is not clear-cut, for locomotives on static display are sometimes put into order for use on preserved lines or on BR excursions.

In past decades, museum preservation of locomotives has been patchy and precarious. The GWR preserved *North Star*, one of its first locomotives, at Swindon Works for many years. Then it was decided it occupied valuable space and Churchward offered it to one of the national London museums, which refused it. It was then scrapped, and twenty years later the GWR built a replica for which, without a blush, it found space in Swindon Works. Of the pre-grouping companies, the North Eastern was the most helpful in locomotive preservation. Its York museum was inherited by the LNER and then BR, which, thanks to their policy of not restricting the collection to NER types, ensured the preservation of the two types of Great Northern Atlantic, the LBSCR 0-4-2 *Gladstone*, and the GWR record-breaker *City of Truro*.

British Railways replaced this rather small York museum with a new one at Clapham, but before long the growing collection was transferred back to York. It did not go to the previous York museum, but to the much

larger and new National Railway Museum, whose main hall was a former roundhouse with tracks converging on to a central turntable. This museum has generated enormous public interest and its still-growing collection is too large to be displayed simultaneously. Some items are in store while others are loaned out for use on preserved lines or excursions. In 1987, the record-breaking LNER streamliner *Mallard* was put into running order by the Museum, and then sent out to haul excursion trains.

Several locomotives of the pioneer age of railways have also been preserved. Stephenson's *Rocket* and *Puffing Billy* are in the London Science Museum, together with Hackworth's *Sans Pareil*. *Locomotion* of the Stockton & Darlington Railway is at York, and a working replica of this machine has also been built.

The Swindon Railway Museum, devoted to the GWR, includes a 'Dean Goods', and a Churchward 'Star' among its exhibits. *City of Truro* was also here, but was later restored for active service both on tourist lines and on BR excursions. Another regional museum is the Glasgow Museum of Transport, which includes NBR and GNSR 4-4-0s in its collection, as well as two celebrated Scottish locomotives, the first British 4-6-0 (the Highland Railway's 'Jones Goods') and the Caledonian 'single' No 123.

ABOVE: *An 0-6-2 tank engine, once used by a colliery railway, at work on the North Yorkshire Moors Railway.*

RIGHT, TOP: *A former GWR 0-6-2 tank engine hauling a tourist train on the North Yorkshire Moors Railway.*

RIGHT: Maude, *an 0-6-0 built for the North British Railway, in charge of a steam excursion at Edinburgh in 1984.*

OVERLEAF: City of Wells, *originally built as one of the SR 'West Country' class, with a steam excursion near Carnforth.*

There are several private railway museums which, apart from their static exhibits, also present locomotives in steam. Those which exhibit large mainline locomotives are the Bressingham Steam Museum in Norfolk, the Birmingham Railway Museum, which provides former GWR and LMS locomotives for mainline excursions to Stratford-on-Avon and Didcot, the Didcot Railway Centre, which also offers GWR engines for excursions, the Dinting Railway Centre, near Manchester, whose ex-LMS locomotives sometimes haul excursions, and the Midland Railway Centre at Butterley, specialising in former MR locomotives.

The Bulmer Railway Centre at Hereford played a key role in the establishment of a steam excursion programme over BR tracks, after years in which BR refused to entertain this idea. It maintained and serviced three mainline locomotives which bore the brunt of such excursions in the 1970s, the GW *King George V*, the LMS *Princess Elizabeth*, and the SR *Clan Line*. More recently, the Steamtown Railway Museum, based on the former LMS Carnforth locomotive dept, has been supplying locomotives.

The tourist railways are the commonest form of railway working museums. Among the best-known is the Bluebell Railway in Sussex, which was the pioneer standard-gauge line whose success in the 1960s stimulated other enthusiasts to establish similar lines elsewhere. The Bluebell Railway specialises in SR locomotives, and is strong in tank locomotives of the SR constituent companies. In northern England the Keighley & Worth Valley Railway is of about the same size, running trains over a five-mile line, and uses mainly ex-LMS locomotives. Also in Yorkshire is the North Yorkshire Moors Railway, which extends for 18 miles from its terminus near Pickering and possesses, among others, several ex-North Eastern Railway freight locomotives.

Comparable to the North Yorkshire Moors Railway in length is the Severn Valley Railway from Bridgnorth to Kidderminster. This has a large stock of GWR and LMS engines and facilities for restoration and heavy repair. Ex-Southern Railway tender locomotives can be seen on one of the more recently-opened lines, the Mid-Hants Railway at Alresford in Hampshire.

These preserved lines are branches, or parts of branches, of the former companies, and make great and successful efforts to preserve the branchline atmosphere. There are many more that cannot be mentioned here, but three ex-GWR branches cannot be ignored: the Torbay and Dartmouth Railway in South Devon, the Dart Valley Railway at Buckfastleigh, and the West Somerset Railway at Minehead. All these use GWR tank locomotives of various types although the first-mentioned also boasts a 'Manor' 4-6-0.

Two kinds of preserved railways do not depend on the branchline atmosphere. These are the narrow-gauge lines, which have their own special ambience, and the 'mainline' Great Central Railway. The latter, centred at Loughborough, is based on part of the old Great Central Railway's main line, and it is hoped to enlarge the preserved section as far as Leicester. This 'London Extension' of the old GCR was Britain's last main line, and is well-engineered and therefore easily maintained. The new, preserved Great Central uses mainly LNER locomotives, including a GCR 'Director' 4-4-0, *Butler Henderson*.

Most of the narrow-gauge lines are in Wales. Oldest among them, and the very first preserved railway, is the

LEFT, TOP: *The Gresley Pacific* Bittern, *painted to masquerade as the pioneer* Silver Link, *at York in 1988.*

LEFT, BELOW: Sir Nigel Gresley, *another preserved A4, with a steam excursion.*

ABOVE: *The record-breaking GWR 4-4-0* City of Truro *hauling an excursion in 1986 on the York to Scarborough line.*

RIGHT: *The LMS lightweight 2-6-2 tank engine No.41241 hard at work.*

seven-mile Talyllyn Railway. Not far away is the Ffestiniog Railway, distinguished for its use of 'Fairlie' double-ender locomotives. The Snowdon Mountain Railway is hardly a preserved line, for it is still performing its original function of taking tourists to the top of Snowdonia, and it might be better termed a vintage railway. The same might be said of the Vale of Rheidol Railway, which was always a scenic railway for tourists. The Llanberis Lake Railway is different in that it uses the tracks of a former quarry railway, while the Bala Lake and the Brecon Mountain railways are fairly recent creations built on former standard-gauge routes. In many ways, the most atmospheric of these Welsh narrow-gauge lines is the Welshpool and Llanfair which, like the standard-gauge Nene Valley Railway at Peterborough, supple-

ments its British locomotives with engines from overseas railways.

Just as the British tourist railways are too numerous to mention individually, so is the list of British preserved locomotives too long to reproduce here. Specialised handbooks, reprinted frequently, are published to serve as complete reference sources both for locomotives and lines. But the following summary should at least show the great variety of classes that have been preserved, and is a fairly exhaustive guide to the larger mainline preserved locomotives.

There are over one hundred preserved GWR locomotives. Many of these are still awaiting restoration by the locomotive societies which own them, but most have a definite completion date in view. Among them are three

ABOVE: *A scene on the Torbay Railway in Devon. The locomotive is a 2-8-0 tank engine, one of a series built by the GWR for hauling short-distance coal trains.*

RIGHT, TOP: *On the Ffestiniog narrow-guage railway in North Wales. The train is hauled by a 2-6-2 tank locomotive built in the USA for service on the Western Front during World War I.*

RIGHT: *A former BR 2-6-4 tank engine at work on the North Yorkshire Moors Railway.*

OVERLEAF: *Former GWR* Dryslwyn Castle *with a steam excursion near Banbury in 1984.*

'Kings', of which *King George V* is active, and two under restoration. There are also eight 'Castles'. of which four are runners although one of these, *Pendennis Castle*, is privately preserved in Australia. There are no fewer than thirteen 'Hall' 4-6-0s, and nine 'Manors'. Among other tender engines are five of the 2800 class 2-8-0, two 2-6-0s, a 'Dukedog' 4-4-0, a 'Dean Goods', a modern 0-6-0 of the 2251 class, and the well-known *City of Truro* and *Lode Star*. The rest are tank locomotives, with large contingents of those most suitable for use on preserved lines.

The preserved ex-LNER locomotives, by contrast, total less than 50 because few of such locomotives were sent to Barry for scrapping. Thus there are many gaps in the collection with such notable types as the Gresley K3 2-6-0 unrepresented. However, the celebrated *Flying Scotsman* was saved by private initiative and, apart from hauling excursions in England, has also performed in the USA and Australia. Of the streamlined Gresley 4-6-2s, six have been preserved, including one in Canada and one in the USA. Of the British examples, *Sir Nigel Gresley, Mallard*, and *Union of South Africa* are in running order and perform frequently on steam excursions. Another LNER 4-6-2, of the post-Gresley generation, is *Blue Peter*, preserved thanks to its connection with a BBC children's TV programme of the same name. Gresley's *Green Arrow* V2 2-6-2 is also in running order. Other Gresley types preserved are his K4 2-6-0, his 4-4-0 *Morayshire* and his 0-6-2 suburban tank engine. Of the LNER constituent companies, the Great Central is represented by one of its famous 04 class 2-8-0s, and the 4-4-0 *Butler Henderson*. The Great Eastern representatives are an F4 2-4-0, a B12 4-6-0, two types of 0-6-0, and a couple of tank engines. Former NER types have survived more strongly. Four freight locomotives, two 0-8-0s and 0-6-0s, have been acquired by the North Yorkshire Moors Railway. The 4-4-0 No 1621, participant in the 'Race to the North', is in the National Railway Museum together with an 1875 2-4-0, while the Darlington Railway Museum has another 2-4-0 and an 1874 0-6-0. There is also an 0-6-0 tank locomotive, one of a series built by British Railways to a NER design. The Great Northern Railway has relatively few survivors. No 1, the Stirling Single, has made several runs since retirement, and so has the small Atlantic *Henry Oakley*. One of the larger Atlantics has also been saved, as well as the aforementioned Gresley 0-6-2 tank locomotive. Of the Scottish constituent companies, the GNSR and NBR 4-4-0s at Glasgow are supplemented by the NBR 0-6-0 *Maude*, which has performed on several steam excursion trains.

About 90 locomotives of the LMS and its constituent companies have been preserved. This total includes no fewer than 14 of the Class 5 4-6-0, an easy-to-maintain and suitably-sized locomotive for excursion work. Of the larger locomotives, two of the earlier Stanier Pacifics have been saved, of which *Princess Elizabeth* is a runner. Three of the later Stanier 4-6-2s have also been saved, with *Duchess of Hamilton* a frequent performer on excursions, *City of Birmingham* on display in Birmingham's Museum of Science and Industry, and *Duchess of Sutherland* at the Bressingham Museum. Four 'Jubilees' and two 'Royal Scots' have also been saved, with three of the former fit for excursion use. Twenty engines of Midland Railway design have been preserved, but half of these are the standard MR 0-6-0 tank whose building was continued by the LMS. The

ABOVE: *A Fairlie 'double-ender' on the Ffestiniog Railway. This type of locomotive, specially designed for the narrow gauge in the 1870s, was pioneered on this Railway, and the tradition was maintained when the line became a preserved railway.*

RIGHT: *The LNER 2-6-0 No.2005 with an excursion near Edinburgh in 1987.*

other MR designs include the compound 4-4-0, a Single, and a 2-4-0. The LNWR is poorly represented, partly because so many LNWR types were scrapped prematurely in the 1920s and 1930s. An 0-8-0 freight engine has survived, but none of the twentieth-century passenger locomotives. Only the 2-4-0 *Hardwicke* represents the late nineteenth-century LNWR passenger engine, although the much earlier Single *Cornwall* has been saved, as has *Lion* of the Liverpool and Manchester Railway and *Columbine* of the Grand Junction Railway. A LNWR 'coal tank' 0-6-2 has also been saved and is in occasional excursion use. Four Lancashire & Yorkshire, three Caledonian, one Highland, one Glasgow & South Western, and one North Staffordshire locomotive represent the other main constituents of the LMS.

More than seventy Southern Railway locomotives escaped the scrapyard, although these are mainly of modern design. No fewer than fourteen of the 'West Country' light Pacifics and nine of the bigger 'Merchant Navys' have been saved, and in the case of the 'Merchant Navys', this means that almost one third of the class has been preserved. One example each of the 'Lord Nelson' and 'King Arthur' 4-6-0 types have been saved, and both have been used on excursions in recent years. Three of the SR 'Schools' 4-4-0 have also been saved, although one of these is in the USA. Five of the mixed-traffic S15 4-6-0s have also been kept, and this type, like the SR 2-6-0 (also strongly represented) is ideal for excursion and tourist line work. Of former LSWR types, the most interesting are two 4-4-0s and a number of 0-4-4 tank engines, as well as older tank engines of the 2-4-0 and

4-4-2 wheel arrangement. The SECR is represented by a Wainwright 4-4-0, two 0-6-0s, a 0-4-4 tank engine and four of the tiny P class 0-6-0 tank engines. The LBSCR, most of whose mainline engines were early victims of electrification, is mainly represented by small tank locomotives, including ten of the small 'Terrier' class 0-6-0 tank engines. But thanks to an inter-war initiative by railway enthusiasts, an 0-4-2, *Gladstone*, has been saved.

In its early years, the nationalised British Railways built a range of new standard steam locomotives for country-wide use, and several of these have been preserved. Seen most often on excursions is the last steam engine built by BR, the 2-10-0 *Evening Star*. Five others of this type have also been saved. Three BR Pacifics have been preserved: two 'Britannias', of which one, *Britannia*, is in running order, and the solitary big 3-cylinder Pacific *Duke of Gloucester*. Interestingly, while the latter was being restored to running order a small but vital mis-assembly by its original builders at Crewe was revealed, and this constructional error was enough to explain the engine's indifferent steam production when in BR service. Altogether, almost forty BR-built steam locomotives have been rescued, the largest

contingent being twelve of the 2-6-4 tank design, well-suited to operation on tourist lines.

In Ireland, *Maeve*, one of the three fine 3-cylinder 4-6-0s built for the Dublin-Cork express service, is among the locomotives exhibited in the Belfast Transport Museum. In addition, the Railway Preservation Society of Ireland organises excursions and rail tours in both parts of Ireland using its own locomotives, including the compound 4-4-0 *Merlin* and the older 4-4-0 *Slieve Gullion*, both of the former Great Northern Railway (Ireland).

Mainline steam excursions in mainland Britain commenced in 1971, three years after the end of steam traction in regular service. In those intervening three years, BR had refused to entertain the idea of steam operations over its own lines, believing that they would inevitably detract from its modern image, as much of BR management fondly thought the absence of steam was proof of modern thinking. But in 1971 *King George V* was allowed to operate to Birmingham, London, and Swindon. It performed well, and marked the beginning of a very extensive programme of subsequent steam runs during the years to follow.

ABOVE: LEFT. *No.4588, a former GWR 2-6-2 tank locomotive, at work on the Torbay Railway. Being designed for lightly-laid, curving lines, this class of locomotive is ideal for many tourist operations.*

ABOVE: *The rolling scenery enjoyed by passengers on the Keighley & Worth Valley Railway. The train is hauled by a former LMS tank locomotive painted in the tourist railway's own colour scheme.*

RIGHT: *Another train on the Keighley & Worth Valley Railway, this time hauled by an 0-6-0 tank locomotive that once belonged to the LMS although essentially of a Midland Railway design.*

STEAM TRAINS PRESERVED

In 1975, the Steam Locomotive Operators Association (SLOA) was set up. Its members were locomotive owners and its purpose was to negotiate with BR, although it also assumed a public relations and marketing function. One of its first tasks was to reach agreement on which BR lines could be used for steam excursions, and eventually, after some experiment, certain lines became established as steam routes. Pre-requisites for selection were a fairly sparse normal train service, so that steam specials would not add to, or cause, congestion and easy access to a depot where steam locomotives could be maintained.

The most frequently used lines are now those over the Welsh Marches from Shrewsbury to Newport, with a connection from Manchester; from Birmingham to Didcot with the lines to Stratford-on-Avon included; from York to Leeds and from Leeds to Carlisle via the Settle & Carlisle line; and from Carnforth to Sellafield. In Scotland, there are additional approved lines, embracing Edinburgh, Stirling, Perth and Dundee among others. There are occasional additions to the approved lines, sometimes for a summer season only. The line from Marylebone Station in London and thence northwards over the old GWR line through Banbury has become popular in recent years, as has the York-Scarborough line. In Scotland, part of the spectacular West Highland Railway now has a regular summer steam service. In some years, to mark particular events, other routes see steam. In the 1985 celebrations to mark the 150th anniversary of the GWR, steam trains ran between Bristol and Plymouth, Swindon and Gloucester, and Swansea and Carmarthen.

Both BR and the locomotive owners organise steam excursions, although there is necessarily close co-operation between the two, because BR has the lines and the owners have the locomotives. One of the most successful of the BR ventures has been the 'Shakespeare Limited' Sunday luncheon express which runs during the summer to provide a steam-hauled excursion from London Marylebone to Stratford-on-Avon. Designed largely with foreign tourists in mind, the fare for this trip is quite high, but a traditional English luncheon is included. For the railway enthusiast, this train provides a chance to see heavy passenger locomotives at work on the former GWR Birmingham main line.

This train uses standard BR coaches, and is normally of eight vehicles. Providing coaches for steam-hauled trains has often presented a problem, because the ideal of running a homogeneous train consisting of vintage coaches is difficult to attain. Although restoration of old railway coaches has continued alongside locomotive restoration, inevitably single vehicles rather than complete trains have been restored. In the early days of preservation, it was possible to assemble a few trains of fairly recent company stock, and there was, for example, a good GWR corridor train set. But the high cost of adapting coaches to BR's changing standards has had the effect of virtually removing former company-owned rolling stock from use on BR excursions, even though the preserved tourist lines still use such vehicles. There is a train of Pullman cars available, but for the most part steam excursions use fairly elderly BR coaches.

LEFT: Lord Nelson, *built in 1926 and once the Southern Railway's newest and biggest express locomotive, enjoys a fresh lease of life hauling excursions in Cumbria.*

RIGHT: *A good example of how the preservation movement has led to locomotives working trains far removed from their former scene of action. Here a GWR 0-6-2 tank locomotive, designed for the Welsh valleys, hauls tourists on the North Yorkshire Moors Railway.*

INDEX

Acknowledgments

The publisher would like to thank Emma Callery the editor, Adrian Hodgkins the designer, Mandy Little the picture researcher, Pat Coward for preparing the index and the agencies and individuals listed below for supplying the illustrations:

Birmingham Reference Library: pages 33(top), 34(main & top)
Colour-Rail: pages 15(top)LM44, 35(bottom) BRS202, 40-1(bottom)BRW402, 79(bottom) BRE559, 93(top)ME82, 100NE1, 101(bottom) SC592, 111(top)RE264, 130(bottom)BRE586, 138(top)BRM740, 140(bottom)BRW481, 141(top) NE28, 152(bottom)SC543, 153(bottom)BRM320, 161(top & bottom) BRE496

John H. Denby: page 53(middle)
Chris Gammel: pages 14(bottom), 15(bottom), 34(bottom right), 48, 109(bottom), 131(top), 139, 175(top), 180, 187(top)
Hulton Picture Company: pages 8, 9, 10(bottom), 11(bottom), 32(top), 49, 56, 63(bottom), 68, 69(top), 79(top), 102(bottom), 106(top), 135(top & bottom), 150-1
Keystone Collection: pages 18(bottom), 32(bottom), 33(bottom), 66(bottom), 72-3, 73(bottom), 74(left), 80-1, 86(both), 88, 89(both), 90(both), 94-5, 96, 97(both), 102(bottom), 104, 106(bottom), 107(bottom), 123, 124(both), 127
K. P. Lawrence: page 43(bottom)
Andrew Morland: pages 108(all 4), 109(top)
National Railway Museum, York: pages 13, 14(top), 19(both), 20-1, 23, 24, 25, 26(left), 27(top), 35(top), 38(both), 40(top left), 42-3, 46, 53(bottom), 54, 58-9, 60, 64-5, 67(top), 74-5, 76(top), 82-3(bottom), 85(top), 87, 106(middle), 107(top), 110(top), 120-1, 134, 144(bottom left), 155(top)
Peter Newark's Historical Pictures: pages 76(bottom), 103(top)
Punch Archive: pages 22, 40(top right), 82(top), 116(top), 130(top), 152(top)
W. A. Sharman: pages 6, 12, 16(both), 36(bottom), 37(bottom), 43(top), 98-9, 105, 131(bottom), 137, 138(bottom), 142, 168-9, 170-1, 172-3, 175(bottom), 176-7, 182-3, 185
Topham Picture Library: pages 10(middle), 67(bottom), 70-1(top), 77, 84(top), 85(bottom), 146
Victoria & Albert Museum, London: page 111(bottom)
John Westwood: pages 10(top), 17(both), 18(top), 30-1, 32(bottom), 39, 41(top), 47(both right), 50-1, 55(both), 57(both), 59(inset), 60, 61, 62-3, 66(top), 78, 84(bottom), 91, 113, 114-5, 117, 118, 118-9, 122(both), 124-5, 126, 128(both), 135(middle), 136(top), 140(top both), 141(bottom), 145, 147(both), 148(both), 149(both), 153(top), 154(bottom), 156, 157(both), 158(both), 159, 160(both), 164(both), 165, 167(top), 181(top)
Wiedenfeld Archive: pages 72(bottom), 83
Jim Winkley: pages 22(bottom), 26(right), 27(both), 29(both), 36-7, 44-5, 53(bottom), 70-1(bottom), 72(bottom), 73(bottom), 101(top), 103(bottom), 112, 132-3, 136(bottom), 143(both, 144(top & right), 154(top), 155(bottom), 162-3, 166, 167(bottom), 170, 174(top), 178(both), 179(both), 181(bottom), 184, 186, 187(bottom), 188, 189
P. Winstanley: page 178(top)

Colour-Rail slides are available for purchase from Ron White, 5 Treacher's Close, Chesham, Bucks HP5 2HD